GOD'S TIME,
GOD'S MONEY

GOD'S TIME, GOD'S MONEY

Fred Catherwood

HODDER AND STOUGHTON
LONDON SYDNEY AUCKLAND TORONTO

British Library Cataloguing in Publication Data

Catherwood, *Sir* Fred
    God's time, God's money.
    1. Christian life
    I. Title
    248.4   BV4501.2

    ISBN 0 340 42889 9

To Jonathan and Alison

Contents

Introduction

I hope that this book will be a *practical* help to those who want to make the best out of their time, talents and money.

We all seem to live in a rush today, with too much to do and too little time to do it all. The Christian feels especially guilty. We know that we are meant to be making the best use of our time and we are forever failing to find time for what we know we ought to do. It is only when the pressure becomes intolerable that we are forced to work to some kind of system. I hope that the book will inspire the reader to work out a systematic use of time before the moment of desperation arrives! We also need to decide how to make the really big decisions about the use of our time, what training we should take, what kind of jobs we should do and where our own basic talents lie.

I have always been deeply impressed by Christ's two parables, the one in Matthew's gospel (Mt 25:14–30) and the other in Luke's (Lk 19:11–27), about the use of talents and the quite ferocious condemnation of the man who will not use his one talent. The sins of commission are obvious, the sins of omission are mostly unseen. Yet we are told in the epistles that each member of the church has their particular talent and, like the parts of a body, each is vital to the whole. So any Christian who fails to use their talent is crippling the church's work and witness.

I have also always been impressed with our own duty to multiply our talents, to use all our resources of mind and body to the full, to learn, train and gain experience to the limit of our capacity. But, like our use of time, this needs to be managed. We need to learn how to learn, we need to know how to make the most of our experiences, how to move into a tougher job without falling flat on our face. Of course, we all have limits and no one should lightheartedly take on work they can't do. But we should always be pressing on the frontiers, making reconnaissances to find out which new frontiers we can still cross.

Those who use their time and talents well do not automatically become rich. The apostles had given up worldly riches. But Paul was an excellent fundraiser, and the church does need money to look after the needy and to spread the gospel. Those who use their time and talents to the full are more likely to be able to supply the church's need.

Our obligation to give comes directly from our obligation to God, the giver of all. If we believe, as Christians should, that God the creator gives us life and all the means of living, gives us intellect, art and beauty, and that God the Son gave us his life and bore the punishment for our sin of rebellion, then our obligation to God is boundless. But though he can demand everything, including life itself, for most of us the demand is only 10%. Yet we quibble about that. We're either too poor or, with progressive taxation, too rich! We say that the tithe is legalistic, and we forget that the logic of that is that we should pay more. Yet God promises to reward those who give and asks us to try it out. Those who do, find that the 90% seems to go further. The obligations are far easier to meet in a tithing church, but they do not end there. We have to give responsibly, through those best able to handle God's money, to those we are sure will use it best.

The proper use of God's time, talents and money separates the men from the boys, those who are serious about their Christian faith from those who are playing at it. It not only helps us to lead a more orderly life, it is absolutely necessary if the church is to make an impact on the world – and the world has never needed it more.

The pioneer missionaries needed to use all their time and talents to plant new churches in Asia and Africa. They also needed, behind them, churches filled with individual Christians who were ready to give. The new pagans are in formerly Christian countries, and we have pressing needs in our own homelands as well as thousands of miles away.

The Christian church is rightly concerned that its love shall extend, as Christ's did, to the whole man, body and soul. We need pioneers in economic development of the same calibre as those who introduced the scientific method 'for the relief of man's estate'. We need once more the reformers who stood against corruption and for the dignity of man. We have new battles to fight, but we have the same need for the time, talents and money to fight them.

I remain an optimist, not because of the state of the world, which is terrible, but because of the vision of the kingdom of God and of the power of God, using ordinary frail mortals who are prepared to trust him and follow where he leads.

1 Time is God's gift

We live next to a very old church, with graves around it dating back over a thousand years. Those gravestones which are not worn down by weather and covered in moss, all record a date of birth and a date of death. Some of those life spans are long and some tragically brief. As we turn off the busy TV at the end of an evening and look out at the moon shining on the old church tower, we remember that no one is here for long.

The question we all need to ask ourselves is, What should we do with our time?

Christians believe that we owe our lives to God our creator and that he has given each of us our lease of life for a purpose. We are not cosmic accidents, we are men and women made in the image of God. We fit into a divine plan. Above all, we are God's servants, here to do what he wants us to do.

Jesus told the apostles, 'whoever wants to become great among you must be your servant' (Mt 20:26). The apostles saw themselves, first of all, as God's servants. The apostle Paul starts off his letter to Titus, 'Paul, a servant of God' (Tit 1:1). James has the same opening phrase; and the apostle Peter uses a similar one in his second letter. Paul spells out to the Corinthians what it means to be a servant, 'You are not your own; you were bought at a price' (1 Cor 6:19, 20). So our time is not our own, it is God's time and we will be asked to account for the way we spend it. Nor do we work on our own, we serve with others, each of us a living part of the body of Christ, which is the Christian church. Paul tells the Corinthians that as each part of the natural body has a function, so has each part of the body of Christ and, as in a human body, each part is dependent on the other. So, if we do not play the part God has given us, the whole body of Christ will be weaker.

These beliefs give the Christian a tremendous sense of purpose in life which is in sharp contrast to the general sense of aimlessness of today's materialistic society. Both of today's great political creeds, communism and capitalism, are about wealth and its distribution, and yet most people have the feeling that there must be something more to life than that. If the wanton vandalism in our cities has any message, it is that life is about more than property. Those who are out of a job in our society feel that if life is just about wealth, then they belong in the trash can. But even those with money are not happy. The writer of Ecclesiastes has said it all: 'Whoever loves money never has money enough; whoever loves wealth is never satisfied with his income. This too is meaningless' (Eccles 5:10).

Yet Christianity does not go to the other extreme. We are not told to withdraw from this wicked world, to sit on a mountain top in mystic contemplation. Natural religion, on the other hand, puts a sharp divide between the spiritual and the worldly. It teaches that the truly religious withdraw from the world and that its material concerns are beneath them. The spiritual is good, the material evil. That is not *Christian* teaching. Paul tells the Thessalonians to attend to their ordinary work: 'Make it your ambition to lead a quiet life, to mind your own business and to work with your hands, just as we told you, so that your daily life may win the respect of outsiders and so that you will not be dependent on anybody' (1 Thess 4:11,12).

In his second letter to them, Paul says, 'when we were with you, we gave you this rule: "If a man will not work, he shall not eat." We hear that some among you are idle. They are not busy; they are busybodies. Such people we command and urge in the Lord Jesus Christ to settle down and earn the bread they eat' (2 Thess 3:10–12).

Paul's advice is very much in line with the Old

Testament. The book of Proverbs has some hard things to say about those who will not work:

> Go to the ant, you sluggard; consider its ways and be
>   wise!
> It has no commander, no overseer or ruler,
> yet it stores its provisions in summer and gathers its
>   food at harvest.
> How long will you lie there, you sluggard?
> When will you get up from your sleep?
> A little sleep, a little slumber, a little folding of the
>   hands to rest –
> and poverty will come on you like a bandit
> and scarcity like an armed man (Prov 6:6–11).

There is another passage from Proverbs which puts it as vividly:

> The sluggard says, "There is a lion in the road,
> a fierce lion roaming the streets!"
> As a door turns on its hinges, so a sluggard turns on his
>   bed (Prov 26:13,14).

Behind the apostolic instructions and the ancient wisdom is a belief, not shared by natural religion, that *one* God created the universe and that despite the obvious presence of evil, God is still sovereign and that the world is still God's world. As he has worked to create it, so we, each as one of his trustees for our own life span, must work to look after his masterpiece. There is no great gulf between religious and material, between spirit and matter. God himself created matter, he organised it by orderly laws in one, rational, uniform, stable system for our express benefit, so that we can classify it, understand it and use it. Mankind's rebellion may have damaged the divine system, but it has not destroyed it – not yet!

Adam was the first trustee of God's creation, 'Then the Lord God took the man and put him in the Garden of Eden to work it and take care of it' (Gen 2:15). Adam's rebellion produced the first great natural catastrophe – and the world has not been the same since – but it did not rescind the trusteeship. After the second great natural catastrophe, God renewed the trusteeship to Noah and his descendants and promised that the natural laws would remain stable from then on and that there would be no further universal cataclysms (Gen 8:21,22; 9:8–17). That promise has been kept and the natural laws remain stable. So *all* work is God's work, whether it is in full-time church service or not. *All* Christians are officers in God's kingdom; *all* our time is God's time and each of us has to know the particular office in which God wants us to serve, the career for which he wants us to train and the particular jobs he wants us to do.

If we accept that our lifetime is one of service in God's kingdom, then each of us has to make up our minds how God wants us to spend the life that he has given us. When we are young we have to decide whether to go for further education, for more practical training, when to get married and start up a family, whether to go to countries with better opportunities. How do we know how God wants us to use our lives?

How does God want me to use my lifetime?

God not only gives the gift of time and all the opportunities to use it, he also shows us which opportunities to take. He has a place for us in his kingdom and he wants to show us what it is. He has a number of ways of doing this.

First of all, *God guides us by events*. Although God wanted the gospel to go abroad to the ends of the earth, the early church was attached to Jerusalem. It was persecution which scattered them, first to Samaria and beyond and finally Jerusalem itself was destroyed by the armies of Titus. The events which dictate to us may not be so dramatic, but they dictate all the same. We fail one exam and pass another, we lose one job and get another. One girlfriend or boyfriend turns us down and another accepts us. One door shuts and another opens.

It is often tough to be guided by events. Joseph was sold as a slave to Egypt and put in prison before he became ruler for Pharaoh. Nothing could have been tougher. But he told his brothers, 'God sent me ahead of you to preserve . . . and to save your lives . . . So then, it was not you who sent me here, but God' (Gen 45:7,8). Daniel, a bright young Jewish prince, was taken prisoner by the Babylonians. Right at the threshold of his career, his life was shattered. That was tough too. The attachment of the early church to Jerusalem was natural. They had all been brought up as Jews and found it very hard to accept that the gospel was not just for the Jews. They had been told to take it to the ends of the earth, but they were inclined to start where they were. Persecution was a hard school, but if the early church had not got out of Jerusalem, most of us would not have heard the Christian gospel.

Seventeenth-century persecution took whole churches out of Europe to found a country with freedom of worship. It is hard for us to have to move out of a place we know and away from those we love, or out of a job into which we've put our time and energy. We are creatures of habit and we have our own ideas and ambitions, so we're not easy to shift. Often it needs events to make us move.

Second, *God surrounds us with advice*. The church is there to help us decide whether we have a call to full-time Christian service. The family is full of advice as to whether this girlfriend or boyfriend is our call to marriage. Those we work with tell us how good we are – and they often tell us our limitations without our asking.

We all do well to listen to good advice. Our own ambition, greed, obstinacy and sentiment give us plenty of bad advice, all carefully concealed and plausibly rationalised. Even our good intentions and youthful enthusiasm can give us bad advice.

When I was at university, I had the enthusiasm which a

lot of young Christians feel for overseas mission. I went to
hear the most enthusiastic missionary I have ever met,
David Bentley-Taylor, and he spelt out the qualifications
needed in a missionary. One by one I realised I didn't have
them: I was not patient, I was not a natural linguist, I found
it hard to put up with continual sickness, I was not naturally
tolerant of the follies of others . . . He also pointed out the
high cost to the missionary society in sending out and
training the wrong people – not to mention the damage
ill-suited missionaries could cause before they were
shipped home again. By the end of the session, I was
quite clear that I did not have the qualifications to be a
missionary.

Anyone who is going to cross the culture barrier needs to
be friendly, outgoing, interested in new people, new customs, new places, new ways of thought, and able to relate
without condescending. Churches should advise tense,
introverted members that they may be earnest Christians,
but are unlikely to make good missionaries. Missionaries
also need to be able to master complex foreign languages –
and the more primitive the language and the less its
idiosyncrasies have been flattened through use by for-
eigners, the more complex it remains. And, just as an
exasperated aside, churches who want to spend good
money in sending enthusiastic kids to roam around, trying
to evangelise in countries where they can't even speak the
language, should have a word first of all with the churches
in the countries who have to receive them. There are better
ways of spending scarce resources.

In your job – and this applies to Christian jobs just as
much as to secular ones – it's good to take advice. The world
is full of ambitious people who have made up their minds
where they are going and who are determined to get there.
Quite often they achieve their ambition, but that is all they
do achieve. On the way they lose friends, families, health
and peace of mind and when they finally get where they
want to be, they find it worthless, hold on to it briefly and
then have nothing more to live for. More often they do not

achieve their goal and become frustrated, cynical and embittered.

Usually those who work alongside us have a more objective view of our capacities than we have, and friends who know us give us more realistic advice than we can give ourselves. No one is ever at the receiving end of their own personality! So none of us ever has quite the measure of ourselves that others do. It is also far easier, when you work in a team, to do the job which the others want you to do than the job you insist on doing against everyone's wishes. The first is tailor-made for success, the other for failure. Oliver Cromwell said, 'That man goes farthest who knows not where he goes.' He was saying that those who are open to going where they are wanted are likely to go further in a lifetime's career than those who insist on trying to impose their own rigid course. Christians, whose aim is service, also need to see what kind of service the world wants – unlike the French politician who, talking of the milk surplus, said that even if the Third World Moslems didn't approve of eating fat, they should get used to it, because the French dairy farmer certainly wasn't going to produce anything else.

Perhaps the most emotional and difficult subject on which to take advice is about choosing our life's partner. But there is nothing more likely to dim a young Christian's enthusiasm for a life of Christian service than a partner in marriage who doesn't see it in the same way. In the controversial passage in Paul's first letter to the Corinthians (1 Cor 7), he says, 'An unmarried man is concerned about the Lord's affairs – how he can please the Lord. But a married man is concerned about the affairs of this world – how he can please his wife – and his interests are divided' (1 Cor 7:32–33). In the context, Paul talks of 'the present crisis' and is probably writing to a church suffering from persecution, where any added responsibility was unwise. But Paul's friends Priscilla and Aquila were clearly of great help to each other and to all their friends, including Paul. The partners in a good Christian marriage, with their mutual help, are far stronger than either of them could be alone. So in planning a life of service, we need to be sure we have a partner with whom we will be both stronger and better able to serve.

In many countries, the parents still choose the marriage partners. Most summers, my wife and I help at an international summer school for Christian students. For the last few years one of the hottest topics has been the position of women in society. The strongest views on women's liberation came, three years in a row, from California and Scandinavia. They were deeply shocked by the defence of arranged marriages, put up one year by a Japanese girl. She said that marriage was a good deal more stable in Japan than it was in California. The consensus usually came down to the belief that we should, one way or another, honour our parents in making the choice and that it certainly meant consulting them, listening to what they said and if they were against a particular choice, considering it most carefully before we committed ourselves.

Of course parents can have ambitions for their children which override their judgement. They can want to hold on to them for selfish reasons. They can be jealous. Yet they usually do want their children's happiness, they do know them very well and they have seen more of the world; even if they do mix the right reasons with wrong ones, we still need to listen. Brothers and sisters also give good advice, and sometimes a friend of the family will help if the family argument gets too tense. But God has certainly put the fifth commandment there for a purpose and Paul pointed to the promise that went with it (Eph 6:2,3).

Third, *God gives us obligations* – family obligations, contractual obligations, moral obligations, church obligations – all of which steer us firmly in one direction or another. I was once offered a job in Vancouver. When I told my wife as I came through the door, she burst into tears. Vancouver was just too far from all our nearest and dearest. Though I badly wanted to leave the job I was doing as soon as I could, a weeping wife on the doorstep put paid to Vancouver.

Looking back over many such decisions, there's no doubt that an existing obligation gives us a most reliable steer. I've never known it fail.

A great many people who want to go into overseas Christian service are prevented by parents who have become dependent on them and cannot be left alone. That is an obligation which has been written into the moral law and which we are not entitled to override. Christ was scathing about the Pharisees, who said, 'Honour your father and mother', but were able to allow people to evade their responsibilities by invoking the idea of *corban*, saying: 'Whatever help you might otherwise have received from me is a gift devoted to God' (Mt 15:3–9). On the cross, Jesus fulfilled his last filial obligation by putting his mother into the charge of the apostle John (Jn 19:25–27).

We are also under an obligation to see that the job we do not only conforms to the moral law, but is worthwhile for a Christian to do. There are a whole range of industries and occupations in which Christians do not normally want to be involved. To put it at its most obvious, no Christian wants to be responsible for selling horror movies or pornographic literature.

And we want the job to be honest. In countries with widespread corruption, it is hard enough for a Christian to find a worthwhile job which is not enmeshed in the web of corruption. I was asked by one young Third World businessman who had become a Christian, what he should do. I suggested that he should concentrate on exports to countries where he did not have to bribe the buyers. This would also protect him at home from official demands for bribes, since every Government would want to encourage businesses earning scarce hard currency. After we had talked, I asked him how he had met the problem so far. He said, 'I've done exactly what you have just suggested. I was in a family business and when I became a Christian, I refused to bribe. After a great argument with my father, we agreed to split the business. He thought it would fail, but it has worked just as you say.'

Sometimes the dishonesty is more subtle. Another young manager was running a public company. It was a tough but satisfying job, until his boss brought his new mistress into the business, put her on the board of a company he was just about to sell in a deal which gave generous compensation to all the directors for loss of office. He then started to test the young Christian manager's loyalty with other deals which were certainly not for the benefit of shareholders. The outside directors told him not to make a fuss; the executive directors thought of their wives and children. The manager had a wife and small children too, but felt guided by the very clear moral guideline of collective responsibility and resigned.

Fourth, *sometimes God guides us by giving us a vision of the work he wants us to do*. This does not have to be something like the vision of the apostle John on Patmos. God grips us with a need, so that we cannot get it out of our minds. It becomes very vivid and pressing. He gave great missionary pioneers a vision of the country to which he wanted to send them – a vision as compelling as the vision he gave to the apostle Paul of the man of Macedonia who was crying out to Paul for help. Hudson Taylor had a vision for the millions in China who had never heard the Christian gospel. Many people had the vision of ending the slave trade and then of ending slavery itself. Others had a vision for the education of the untaught masses, whom many believed to be un-teachable.

Just before World War Two, a number of Christians in different countries had a vision for an international student movement which would work among the future leaders of all the countries of the world. World War Two put a stop to it, but immediately afterwards they met again and out of that meeting has emerged the International Fellowship of Evangelical Students.

One of those with that vision for students had experienced a vision for his own future several years earlier when he was a young doctor, working for the King's official physician in London – and widely expected to succeed to his practice. The more he diagnosed his rich patients, the more he realised that their real problems were not physical but spiritual and that there was little that he could do for them as a doctor. He became convinced that he should spend his life in passing on his own new-found faith. His medical colleagues tried to dissuade him, but they finally accepted and respected his convictions and he left London's West End with his new wife to become pastor of a working-class church in South Wales. So started Dr Martyn Lloyd-Jones' ministry.

People with this kind of vision are pioneers, they are breaking the mould and have to have very special qualities. But all of us can, in one way or another, have a vision of the need which our particular gifts are meant to meet. There are a great variety of gifts in the church, some spectacular, some not so obvious. One of these, Paul tells the Corinthians, is given to 'those able to help others' (1 Cor 12:28). I like that. It is one of the most useful, though most unobtrusive, gifts in the Christian church.

After God has guided us in various ways, he gives us an inner conviction as we finally come to our decision. With some it has to be a very powerful conviction, to steel them against the opposition they face. The prophet Jeremiah had a particularly rough time. His life was threatened. He was thrown into a dungeon. The king cut up Jeremiah's letter to him page by page and threw it into the fire. No one wanted to hear his bad news that Jerusalem was doomed. Yet he kept on. He said, 'The word of the Lord has brought me insult and reproach all day long. But if I say, "I will not mention him or speak any more in his name," his word is in my heart like a fire, a fire shut up in my bones. I am weary of holding it in; indeed, I cannot' (Jer 20:8,9).

Others may not need that inner conviction quite so much, but we all need it at times when the going is tough, when we ask ourselves why we ever took the job on. At that point we need to be able to retrace our steps and remember the guidance point by point – to see that there was no other way, that we were held inexorably to the course on which we had set out. As we are do this, whatever the problem, we will get a renewed peace of mind and assurance that we are in the work to which God has called us.

2 Time flies

Where does all our time go?

We in the industrial democracies work fewer hours than mankind has ever worked before – and yet we are forever short of time. Where does it all go?

If you use a watch and a notebook to account for it all, you will be surprised to discover where it does go. I've twice done this, each time over several weeks, and the results were not at all what I'd imagined. I reckoned an hour between rising and leaving the house. It was twenty or thirty minutes longer. I never started the first job in the morning as soon as I imagined. Lunchtime breaks took much longer than I had thought. And I never made up the time in the evening. But it is in the seventy or more hours a week that we are not at work and not asleep that the biggest surprises come. Where *does* it all go?

TV time
We know, because the advertising companies log it for us, that an enormous amount of time goes in watching TV. Some watch as much as five hours a day, that is thirty-five hours a week; 1,820 hours a year. That is very nearly a third of our waking time in front of the set, over twenty years of our lives. Maybe it is only three hours of our time and only fourteen or fifteen years of our lives. Why not put a watch on it and measure it? And while we're about it, why not analyse what you are watching?

TV has done a lot for us. No one at home knew the horror of the slaughter in World War One. Vietnam was different. The blood came right into the home. I remember too seeing

the Kennedy–Nixon debate – the first time in a presidential
election when the camera could cut away all the rhetoric
and get down to the real argument. I have a feeling that
Hitler would not have come over too well on TV. *All the
President's Men* was worth the hours spent in front of the
set. Each of us has a memory of TV 'greats'. The rest
mercifully fade from the memory. But it is the rest which
take the time.

I have a job which almost totally eliminates time in front
of the small screen – unless you count a rapid switch, while
undressing, round Brussels' fifteen channels, comparing
westerns dubbed in French with those dubbed in German
('levez les mains' sounds too elegant to be credible!). So I
can assure readers that there is a perfectly reasonable life
without TV.

Another large chunk of our time goes in reading news-
papers. Here I plead guilty. That's where the time goes
before I leave home and the daily press competes with time
I ought to spend in prayer. I argue that my job as a politician
needs it, and there's something in that. But I often wonder,
when I've read all the political columns, whether I'm any
the wiser. And having for a long time now been in the
business of releasing news and watching its treatment by
the media, I do know how much is trivialised and slanted,
how much of what is important is omitted and how much of
what is unimportant is included. The owners are in the
business of selling papers and they are strongly tempted to
print what people want to hear, to run with the tide of
opinion and not against it. The exceptions are the financial
papers, whose readers want the real news because their
money depends on it. But at least you can select the
papers you read and skim the pages for what you need to
know.

Travelling time

Travelling, especially in urban society, takes a great deal of
our time. Recently, with one of our sons, we worked out
how long it would take to commute from home to a new

job. At peak-hour traffic, it totalled one and a half hours each way, or fifteen hours a week. We all agreed that that was too long, but it is not unusual. There are of course arguments for and against living in the middle of cities, but travel time is a powerful argument for city-centre living and if more people insisted on living in city centres, they would become more livable places and a lot of the arguments against living there would fall away.

Some of us also have to spend a lot of time travelling beyond the daily commuter run. When I was elected for a second five-year term to the European Parliament, I reckoned to spend five hundred hours of it in airports. I learnt to cut that down. I never put anything in the hold, always take an aisle seat as far forward as possible for quick getaway, know where to find the spaces in the airport car-park and time my arrival at the airport with the final call for our regular flights. I also spend a bit of time checking on reliable routes and reliable airlines and never fly to America via New York, where we have to waste hours lined up at immigration.

When I drive, I read the local maps and learn where to cut off the motorway before it jams. On our family visits to the Austrian Alps, we quickly learnt that the Munich-Salzburg autobahn jams in the summer about twenty kilometres out of Munich and that, when you've survived that, the wait on the Austrian border can take an hour. So we have perfected a route through all the pretty Bavarian villages which no one else seems to have heard of.

Time spent socialising
Man, the Bible tells us, was not made to live alone, so we spend a lot of time in company. Sometimes we just look in on one other. Sometimes someone throws a party. Friendship is healthy and natural, but we should know whether it is in proportion to everything else. The log will tell us that too. Most Christians will avoid the excesses of all-night parties with too much drink and heavy hangovers which obliterate the next day. But those who are young

enough not to be stopped in their tracks by sheer exhaustion during the evening can be tempted by good company to go on far longer than they intended and, if it is a Friday or Saturday night, to sleep on the next day. Those who enjoy company and whose company is enjoyed by others, will be under pressure to spend more time socialising than they should. The log should tell the true record and put our socialising into perspective.

Time on the phone

What we don't do face to face, we can do on the phone. Those of us who have had teenage children who believe that the phone is as free as running water, know from the phone bills the time they spend in talking to each other. On the other hand, there are church members with a telephone ministry, who spend their time listening to and encouraging those who are in trouble. The log is neutral, but if we find it tells us that we are spending a lot of time on the phone, we should split the record between calls which are necessary and those which are optional.

The other problem, especially with incoming calls, is that they interrupt and, if there are a lot of them, we can spend half our time – I'm not exaggerating – in picking up the threads of our work. Some people take the phone off the hook or switch ruthlessly to an answering machine and call everyone back. But if everyone else did that, communication would be much more difficult. Of course there are more elegant ways of staying free from interruption. I once called a duke to ask him to take on a public service post. The first time, the castle housekeeper answered and said His Grace was out hunting, but the hunt had been sighted from a tower and was thought to be heading home. I waited until early evening and tried again. This time it was the butler. He said in tones of regret, but with great finality, 'His Grace has gone in to dinner.' For some time after, whenever the phone rang during a meal at home, one of our family would say, 'Tell them that His Grace has gone in to dinner.' (The duke did finally show – 'I understand you had a little trouble in getting in touch' – took the job on and did it very well.)

Time looking for lost property
A surprising amount of time goes in doing things which, with a bit of thought, we shouldn't have to do at all. This includes all the time spent in looking for what we've lost or, if it is not really lost, is not immediately to hand. I always try to travel with two keys for the car. If you can't find one in a hurry, there's always the other to hand. If one is really lost, you don't have to spend hours phoning garages or getting the spare one from home. Those of us who travel usually have a short check-list as we set out from home – tickets, passport, money – and we pack our bags to a pattern, so that anything missing is immediately noticed.

There are people who keep untidy rooms and desks and tell us that provided no one else moves anything, they know where everything is. I doubt it. Logically the best way of making sure that you can lay your hands on anything you want in a hurry is to keep a tidy desk, tidy drawers, a tidy room and a tidy home. 'A place for everything and everything in its place' may sound trite and a bit prissy, but it certainly saves time.

One sure way of losing vital documents, books or other possessions is to have too many of them. We are a sentimental family and accumulate lots of objects which are totally useless but remind us of some happy time. We hate to junk anything and, since we have a large old rambling house, everything finds a place somewhere. But where! Somewhere my old yellow rowing cap is tucked away. There's an old trunk in the attic to which we've lost the key and no one can remember what is in it. Books pile up everywhere. Old magazines crowd the cupboards. Mum fights a losing battle against the accumulated possessions of three generations. So if you put something down for five minutes to answer the phone it disappears. It is visible but, like a fallen leaf, indistinguishable.

Learn a fast routine for daily chores

Though the analysis will give us a lot of ideas on where to
find time, it will not show us how to save time on the
minimum of time-consuming chores we all have to do
every day. But we can save time on almost all of them, just
because they are repetitive jobs.

At the end of the last war I was training on twenty-five-
pounder guns. The war ended and we never fired them in
anger, but I did learn how to do a fast drill for repetitive
chores. We could get three guns off their trailers, lined up
and ready to fire in so many seconds because we didn't
have to think about every next action. It was a well-
thought-out, much-practised drill and we did it automatically. That's the way to deal with all repetitive jobs. And if
they're similar but not exactly repetitive, it's good to have
a system.

Shortly after we were married, I went with my boss to see
a film on what was then known as 'time and motion study'.
For some reason our wives came with us, and it so
happened that the film illustrated the idea by domestic
examples. My young wife was fascinated and her quickness
at housework is always put down to the simple illustrations
she saw then – never make two journeys when, with a
moment's thought, you could make one; while one thing is
cooking, get on with something else; always figure out the
quickest order in which to do jobs.

One of our family read that the great missionary pioneer
in China, Hudson Taylor, because he had been horrified at
the total length of time he took each year just to get dressed
and undressed, had worked out the quickest method to do
each task. As a result of this inspiration, no one in the
family can now dress as fast.

Of course we don't always save time for such excellent
reasons. At school, my boarding house was next to the
main classroom block and it took about three seconds
running from door to door. Our first class, before breakfast,
was at 7.45. I got up with the five-minute bell and had time

to grab a cup of cocoa and a biscuit before getting to my desk dressed and on time.

Rhythm instead of rush

There's a great difference between saving time and rushing. We rush when we have not saved enough time to meet a deadline, when we are trying to do more than can be properly done before the deadline. Things done in a rush are things not properly done. A last-minute rush is a sign of failure to plan our time. We drive too fast and risk accidents, we cut corners in our work, we give people who need our time a harsh brush-off, we panic and make mistakes and, even if we succeed, we end up physically and emotionally exhausted.

But even if we do not rush, physical exhaustion is still a limit on the use of our time; and the more tightly we control our time, the more conscious we are of that limit. As a runner and an oarsman, I learnt that one of the secrets of using energy is to learn how to pace yourself. We learnt never to rush, but to find the rhythm which would give us the fastest overall time. The hard drive of the oar through the water was followed by a loose relaxed swing forward, giving us the pause before the next hard drive. In a race on the winding Cam, we'd set ourselves short-term objectives – first-post corner, then grassy corner, then Ditton corner, then the long reach to the railway bridge and the final burst to the finish. If we'd had the finish in our minds from the start, we'd never have kept up the pace.

In life we need the same sense of rhythm. There are times at which we need the hard drive, but if we try to keep that tense energy the whole time, we will exhaust ourselves. We need to balance drive with just the right length of relaxation so that when we drive, we can give it all the punch it needs. We need to give ourselves short-term objectives to keep going for the long term. The apostle Paul reminds us that we are all runners in a race, we need to keep in training, not carry too much weight and keep on course (1 Cor 9:24–27).

Of course we all have our own individual metabolism and our own rhythm. For instance, some are early birds and some are late. To some it is all a matter of springing out of bed at the crack of dawn and doing a day's work before anyone else is up; and there's a lot to be said for that if your metabolism lets you do it. Jesus rose 'a great while before day' (Mk 1:35 RSV) and went out to a lonely mountain to pray. During the day he was surrounded by crowds and it was the only time he could be alone to pray. But those who get up early also need to go to bed early. Though some need less sleep than others, we can't burn the candle at both ends. On the other hand those with a sluggish metabolism need time to get going and claim that they do their best work late at night. Whatever our metabolism, we tend to do our best work when we are fresh. Even those of us who take time to get going are freshest in the first part of the day, so we should tackle the tough jobs first and not leave them until we are tired.

We can all make lots of time for our first priorities if we want to. The next question is, What should those priorities be?

3 Time for what?

Time with God

The first great commandment is that we should love the Lord our God with all our heart, all our mind, all our soul and all our strength (Deut 6:5; Mk 12:28–34). So, in deciding priorities for our time, Christians must put God first. For Christ himself, this meant going out to a mountain alone, long before dawn, to pray to the Father. If that was important for the holy Son of God, it must be even more important for the rest of us. We succumb regularly to all kinds of temptations, but, despite that, we are a great deal more confident that we can cope successfully with whatever stress and temptation the day may bring.

All Christians need time to pray, time to listen and time to think, so that God can set our priorities. The Christian does not come to prayer and meditation with a vacant mind. Our prayer to God is guided by what God has already said. We need time each day to read what our creator has told us. We cannot understand the Christian message by reading snippets of the Bible, phrases which we can only half understand. We need to go on until we really understand how one author complements another and what they are all saying together. We need to study systematically, because the great pillars of truth are mutually supporting, like the columns and arches of a great cathedral, and one truth is balanced by another truth. Paul tells us that we are saved by faith alone and not by works (Rom 3:28; Eph 2:8,9). But as James tells us, 'faith without deeds is dead' (Jas 2:26). So we cannot behave as we like, because true faith changes our lives and makes us want to obey God's law.

God's word is the only reliable guide to the mysteries of good and evil, right and wrong. Listen to the psalmist,

> O how I love your law!
> I meditate on it all day long.
> Your commands make me wiser than my enemies,
> for they are ever with me.
> I have more insight than all my teachers,
> for I meditate on your statutes.
> I have more understanding than the elders,
> for I obey your precepts.
> I have kept my feet from every evil path
> so that I might obey your word.
> I have not departed from your laws,
> for you yourself have taught me.
> How sweet are your words to my taste,
> sweeter than honey to my mouth!
> I gain understanding from your precepts;
> therefore I hate every wrong path. (Ps 119:97–104)

Reading God's word leads on naturally to prayer. When God speaks, we want to speak back to him. And, as we speak, the words we have just read come alive. We read about the widow giving all she had (Mk 12:41–44) and it is just a story. Then we pray and realise our own need to be generous. We read, 'Unless the Lord builds the house, its builders labour in vain' (Ps 127:1) and it dawns on us that we need to rethink our busy self-centred schemes. Those of us who have been Christians for a very long time, see this dialogue with an unseen God as the strong, unbreakable and ever-guiding thread in a changing and uncertain life.

Those who are not Christians may like to believe that this is all in the imagination. But those of us who, over the years, have seen real issues weave in and out of our prayers, connecting the dialogue to events and events to the dialogue, know that both sides of the dialogue are as real as the events to which they relate. Once might be a coincidence, but thirty thousand times could not be.

Answers to prayer are not magical, they are moral; they are always consistent with the moral pattern in God's word. The promises we read there are true and the warnings are also true. In our dialogue with God, he uses the warnings and promises as red and green lights to guide us – and that guidance is always reliable.

The quality of prayer and the time spent in prayer are one of the points of division between the nominal Christian and the real one. The real Christian believes that there is a God 'out there' and that, through our faith in Christ, we have access to the one all-wise, all-powerful being in the universe. Time spent in prayer, through Christ to God, is time spent with the one being who has real power. But it is also time spent with the one who knows us better than we know ourselves and who can be trusted absolutely to give us the wisdom we need to chart our way through the hazards of life. Time spent in prayer saves us from time wasted in the follies of a self-centred life.

We all know that if we are with someone whose good opinion we value, we find ourselves behaving better and being more ready to listen, ready even to accept that we may be wrong. We listen too to those who love us because we know that what they tell us really is for our benefit. When the Christian is at prayer, vanity shrivels, self-assertion creeps away into a corner and, as we get older in the faith, the memory of the faithfulness of God to those who have been prepared to trust him is very vivid.

Prayer is not a ritual incantation, it is a dialogue. God speaks to us through the written revelation. We speak to God, first in worship as we remember who he is, then in response to his words which we have just read and then in thanks for what he has given us, then in request for what is on our minds. And in among our thanks and requests come the moral signposts which God places in our consciousness to show us the way forward.

But prayer is more than the sensible man's time to think through the problems ahead. When we see what we have to do, God helps us to do it. And if we do what is right, he looks after all the other problems, especially the problems of the people who loom so largely and ominously in our lives, who stop us doing what we think we ought to do.

That brings us to our next priority – to spend time with people.

Time with people

The family is the first and the most basic institution given by God, but today the family is breaking up because we have no time for each other. A husband has only one wife, given to him by God, because 'it is not good for . . . man to be alone' (Gen 2:18). A wife has only one husband to cheer her and care for her. I love the section of the Mosaic law which exempts a newly-married man from military service for a year so that he can be at home and cheer up 'his new wife' (Deut 24:5). But we always need to be able to talk to our spouse, to share our burdens with the one person with whom we can be totally secure, who will encourage and support us, but who will also be able to point out gently and kindly where we might be wrong!

With nearly one marriage in two destined for divorce and with more frequent divorces inside the church itself, Christians need to work at their marriages and, above all, to give time to their partner. In every decision we make, as to what kind of job we should do, where we should live, what recreations we have, what commitments outside home and work we take on, we need to look at the result on our time together with our spouse.

I had a friend who was a brilliant golfer, captaining the Cambridge University team. He hoped to teach his new wife the game, so that they could play together. After a few lessons, they went on their first round with each other and at the end, she asked his expert advice. He said, 'Sell the clubs.' But if his wife could not play, he would not play either, so he gave it up too; he would not make her a golf widow.

My wife once met a diplomat in New Zealand whose wife was a partner in a law firm in London. His wife lived in London which had been his last posting. She had been offered a partnership in the law firm in which she worked and knew that if she went with her husband to New Zealand, she was not likely to get another offer. He knew that, if he accepted New Zealand, the next posting would be an embassy of his own and if he refused, he would never reach the peak of his profession. Both put their careers before marriage; but in the Christian social order there are unavoidable obligations about marriage to which career decisions must be subordinate.

We not only have golf widows and career widowers (and vice-versa), we have Christian widows and widowers too. It is easy enough for Christians to fill their evenings with church commitments. The saintly lay preacher who will always accept a speaking engagement can leave at home a lonely wife and bitterly resentful children. God guides us by the duties he has given us and we neglect our family duties at our peril.

Our children have only one father and one mother. They need both. Children need to be able to talk to their parents. They have to have someone who has time to listen, even if it is late at night and weary parents want to go to sleep. We may think that there is a great deal in the world which is more interesting than the prattling of little children or the wild opinions of older ones, which are held so dogmatically that it hardly seems worth arguing with them. But who else would we like them to listen to? If we've not listened ourselves, we can hardly complain if some of the wild ideas are acted out. And it is worthwhile. As they grow older, we realise with amazement that they have actually been listening to us all the time, have been watching to see how what we say matches with what we do, comparing our ideas with the ideas of others and making the same judgement. As the father of a family where communication has been non-stop since our oldest learnt to talk nearly thirty years ago, I would not have it otherwise!

Grandparents are great listeners too. They are at one remove from the immediate discipline of family life, can take a more relaxed attitude and children will open up and say what they might not dare to say to their parents. Some years ago, two friends of ours, Wes and Becky Pippert, were asked to Sunday lunch at the White House by the Carters. Their main memory is of the only other guests, the Carter grandchildren, who dominated the whole occasion. Though one went over the top and had eventually to be removed, it was clear that the President of the United States and the First Lady did not allow the time pressures of the presidency to get between them and their grandchildren.

There are obligations to grandparents too, especially to those who have lost husband or wife and to those who are elderly and cannot go about on their own. Too many old people are shut off without company, parked in old folk's homes or in geriatric wards of big hospitals. When we were weak, they gave us their time and energy. They got up at nights. They sat with us when we were ill. They listened to our nonsense. Now it is their turn. Those with whom they can share memories become fewer and fewer. They can still share them with sons and daughters, laughing at what they did together forty years ago.

The writer to the Hebrews tells us that Christians are not to neglect the times when they get together with each other (Heb 10:25). Time for worship is part of the time we need to give to God. But if we arrive at the last moment and go with the benediction, we cannot in any real sense be part of that fellowship of Christians which we call a church, for we need to know each other and knowing takes time.

A Christian church is a remarkable cross section of the community. There are little old ladies worried about their wills, widows who do not know how to live on their incomes, deserted wives, those who are mentally sub-normal (of whom a sympathetic church should have a large number), drop-outs who smell, young people who want to talk about careers, students with theological posers, nurses who want to know whether to join a trade union, old folk

living in institutions to whom the Sunday at church is the
one bright spot in the week and swarms of children who
want to tell you their latest joke. Even behind the façade of
the average adult with a normal job and adequate income
are all kinds of anxieties which need to be shared with
someone who will listen.

Some members of the church have a special ministry in
giving a sympathetic ear to those who are worried. My
wife spends long hours on the phone and we in the family
do not begrudge it, because we know that she can help so
many people. On Sundays after church, she is the last
person to leave as the deacons shut the doors, because
there is always someone else who wants to talk to her.
There is a real art in listening. We all know the person who
is only waiting for you to stop talking so that they can start.
But there is much more of that in most of us than we like to
admit. It's remarkably easy to conduct an entire conversation without telling the other person anything at all, even if
they have come specifically to ask your views. All you have
to do is to turn the subject of the conversation back to them.
Try it out and see! And then ask yourself whether you ever
do the same. There is a great scarcity of people who have
time to listen, time to reassure, time to comfort, time to
persuade us gently that, just possibly, we may be wrong. I
remember, when I was in my late teens, a friend of my
parents, Tom Rees, sitting up with me until four in the
morning, while I struggled with a decision I knew I ought
to make and wouldn't. And when, a couple of months
later, he thought I was going to go back on the decision I
had finally made, he gave me another four hours of his
desperately limited time.

Christians are told to be hospitable. Those of us who have
homes are to share them. Of course there are limits. David
Watson, the charismatic evangelist, came home to York
from a long trip overseas to find his house full, his study
taken over by students and his library in disarray. He was
very angry and then reproached himself for it. But common
sense tells us that a busy minister needs at least one place he

can call his own. And children need to feel that their home
is their own, a place where they have more claim on their
parent's attention than any stranger in the house.

But while our home should not be swamped, the
Christian house should be an open house where other
members of the church are welcome and where those who
live far away can find a home from home. There is nothing
more comforting to those of us who have to travel than to
know that wherever we go in the world, we can find
hospitality at a Christian home. Those who lend homes for
the church's house groups, for evangelistic Bible studies,
for visiting preachers, for students (and especially for overseas students) are doing a key work in the church. There are
many people who, while not willing to go to a church, will
go to a Christian home.

Although too many visitors may swamp the family,
children in a home with a steady stream of visitors learn a
great deal more about the wide world than those who never
see a stranger. I can remember vividly all the characters
who came to my parent's home; Rev W. P. Nicholson, the
fiery Ulster evangelist, who had led the revival there in the
twenties; Robert A. Laidlaw, the outstanding New Zealand
businessman and Christian leader, with whom I used to
argue fiercely in my teens, but who made an enormous
impact on us all; Tom Rees, the evangelist of the forties and
fifties, who used to fill the Albert Hall; not to mention my
father-in-law Dr Martyn Lloyd-Jones and his wife Bethan,
who first came to stay with us in 1949, five years before I
married his older daughter. And our own children have
friends all round the world from among the students who
have been to the international summer schools at which we
have been house-parents. The hospitality of the Christian is
repaid a hundred times over.

Time for rest

The Christian is in the world as well as the church, and we
have to find time and energy to serve our neighbours too.

Our work, even though we are paid for it, should be done as a form of service. No Christian should regard work simply as a means of making money. We do it to help our fellow men and women. It is an essential part of the Christian duty of care. The book of Proverbs (Ch 6:6–11) tells us not to be slothful and to do whatever we have to do with enthusiasm and energy. The apostle Paul tells us to work hard so that we lack nothing and have enough over to give to those in need (Eph 4:28). And a much-overlooked part of the ten commandments says, very positively, 'Six days you shall labour and do all your work' (Exod 20:9). The fourth commandment is, of course, better remembered for telling us to rest one day a week. God has built into human life the weekly rhythm of one day's rest in seven. It is not an afterthought, it is a creation ordinance, given to man from the beginning of time. It was not just for the Jews or for the church – everyone needs it. Nor is it just a command to take any seventh of our time off work. There is all the difference in the world between taking twenty-four hours off duty when everyone else is working and a whole day when no one in the community is at work. Christians are not being legalistic in trying to keep their community closed down for one whole day a week, since it is for the community's own health. In the competitive world in which we live, businesses have to close together. There are six days in which to buy and sell and that should be enough in any community.

Those Christians whose jobs put them under mental and physical pressure know the blessed relief of a day in which their conscience tells them to switch off completely. They take no business calls, do no work at home on office papers, and no travelling. If they are students they do no study or revision: at midnight on Saturday the papers are put away and do not come out again until Monday morning. They have a physical rhythm of work and rest which would save those who work straight through until they collapse, shattered by nervous exhaustion. They never give themselves time to switch off, are never able to recuperate body and mind, never able to step back and see things in a wider perspective and never have time for their family. A Japanese businessman came to our church, rebelling against the edict of the great 'ziabatsu' for which he worked, that Sunday was to be devoted to golf with the company's most important customers. Sir Henry Royce, designer of the famous Rolls-Royce, said that he was far too busy to take Sunday off and was forced to spend many years of his life confined to bed as an invalid.

Of course Christ tells us that there are to be exceptions. 'The Sabbath was made for man, not man for the Sabbath' (Mk 2:27). He says that if people are taken ill, they must be healed, and if a farm animal falls into a hole, it has to be pulled out (Mt 12:9–13). We can think of present-day examples. We should not be so pedantic about Sunday travel that we wait until midnight before setting out. But we should not let long journeys eat regularly into our Sunday evenings. Sometimes there is a crisis which genuinely cannot wait until Monday. But, while allowing a common-sense interpretation, Christians should fight against the transformation of the one public holiday a week, the day when all the family can be together, into just another working day. Sunday is there today to protect the worker against exploitation by consumerism, just as much as it used to be there to protect the slave and serf against their masters.

For the Christian, Sunday is much more than a day of rest. It is the day when we get our head up from the coal-face, the computer, the production line, the drawing board, the till and the classroom and think of the God who made us and redeemed us. It is the day when the whole church can meet together, when the family are at home and when we have time to read of and think about the eternal spiritual kingdom to which we also belong.

We also need to think of the rhythm which God has built into nature. We are not meant to work day and night. Days were meant for work and night for rest. For the manual worker, through most of human history and in most countries even today, darkness brings a welcome relief to a day of hard labour. Although in countries with cheap electric power, people can now work and play day and night, it is still against the natural order and will sap our strength and do us damage.

Time to think

One of the casualties of the pace at which we live life today is time to think. We come straight home from work to be taken over by the entertainment industry. Leisure time is dominated by TV and, if we're not careful, every spare minute of our day can be taken over by organised leisure of one kind or another. So, not having time to think ahead, events take over and dominate us and we lose the initiative in life – someone else does the thinking and we can only react to what has already happened.

Christians, above all people, should not allow themselves to be carried along by the tide of worldly events, to be dominated without thought by worldly attitudes. When we look at another society, past or present, we wonder why those who live in it never stop to think about where they are going. Why did the Christians in Germany not stop to think about where the Nazis were taking their country? Why do Christians in South Africa not think as we do about apartheid? How did Christians come to be identified with imperialism? Of course there were minorities in the church who did think and did protest; but why were they in a minority?

Or, to take it at a lower level, how do Christians drift into temptation and allow themselves to do things which half a moment's thought would tell them were quite wrong? The apostle Paul tells us to examine ourselves (2 Cor 13:5); it is an exercise we should all go through regularly and systematically. Self-examination is not the same as obsessive and unhealthy introspection. It is a healthy and productive exercise. We all need to look from time to time at our

personal relationships and ask ourselves whether we are
being as helpful to those around us as we should be,
whether we are spending as much time as we should with
our families. We should look at the way we are spending
our time and energy and ask ourselves how much we are
wasting, whether we could be making better use of the gifts
God has given us. We should ask ourselves honestly about
the true motives for our priorities. Is it a real anxiety to see
all our talents, or is it greed or naked ambition?

We should meditate when we pray, especially when we
have to make major decisions, and we should discipline
ourselves to think as much about the impact of our
decisions on others as we think about their impact on
ourselves.

4 Time to train

However tough the job which God gives us to do, he will always match the job with the means to do it. But these means do not come by magic. They come in the ordinary way by long and hard training. We may have a vision of a great work of God. We may feel called to be a missionary at the far ends of the earth and we want to be there at once. But that is not the way God works. We have to put in the time to train.

We all find training irksome and for the best possible reasons. We want to get on with the job. The missionary wants to get out in the field, the student at the theological college wants to preach. The medical student wants to take the surgeon's knife. And with the great increase in professional knowledge, training for a profession takes longer. The demand for second degrees grows. And a lot of our contemporaries are in jobs, earning far more than we do.

Training is very hard work. Making the mind work is hardest of all. We are continually up against the limits of our mental capacity, stretching our powers of thought, logic, reason and memory further than they have ever gone before, working at problems we have never had to solve before. A good many people can't stand it. A student at the great accountancy firm where I served my time got further and further out of his depth. He didn't come in one Friday. On Monday morning the senior manager on the job got a brief telegram from him, 'HAVE SEEN PRICE WATER-HOUSE AND AM NOT RETURNING.'

The institutionalised discipline of training can rub too.

My wife said to a cadet at West Point military academy, 'What is the first year like?' He looked at her, paused and said, 'Hell ma'am.' The chaplain later told us that, despite the prestige of West Point, there was a very high proportion of dropouts in the first year. No doubt the US army believe that it is better that they should crack up then than when they are in charge of troops in the heat of battle.

Those in training also feel that they are not pulling their weight in the world. There comes a time when we want to stop playing and start the real thing. The extension of education well into the twenties is a strain. There comes a time when we have had enough of the theory and we want to get on with the job.

But the hardest training to bear is that given by God when the whole course of our lives is changed by some disaster. It may be war or sickness, exile or even imprisonment. In a world in which knowledge is everything, we find it hard to go through the experiences which God sends us to bring patience, sympathy and wisdom. Academic training is only one kind of training. God has all kinds of ways of training and teaching his servants. Let's look at four cases.

Joseph

Joseph was a favourite son of his father Jacob, conscious from an early age that he had a destiny as a ruler. But he was sold to Ishmaelite traders by his jealous brothers.

His first training was as a slave in an Egyptian house, where his work was so good that he was put in charge of the whole household and learnt to run a small establishment. Then, on a false charge, he was put in prison, where his powers of administration were so outstanding that we next find him in charge of the much larger establishment of the prison, where Pharaoh sent his political prisoners. From them, no doubt, Joseph also learnt something about the administration of Egypt. It was from there that he was finally taken before Pharaoh on the advice of a pardoned prisoner and such was the insight which God gave him that Pharaoh appointed him over the kingdom. And his success in that job enabled him to ask Pharaoh to accommodate his whole family in the land of Goshen where, over four hundred years, Israel grew into a nation.

At any point Joseph might have been discouraged; he might have thought that God had forgotten him, decided that the work of a slave was beneath him and done no more than he need to keep out of trouble. But he believed that God was with him and that he should do as well as he could in the job he had. He might have been even more discouraged to be put in prison on a false charge, but there too, he believed that, despite all appearances to the contrary, God was with him and that he should work as hard as he could. When he met his brothers again, he told them, 'It was not you who sent me here, but God.'

Moses

Moses is one of the greatest men in the Bible. He led the children of Israel out of Egypt to the promised land. It was an extraordinary feat of leadership. But he was not allowed to do this great work of his life until he was eighty. The first forty years of his life were spent as a prince in Egypt, the centre of civilisation in those days. He lived with the country's rulers and judges and learnt the work of the ruler and lawgiver. He would also have learnt all that the Egyptians knew about medicine and hygiene. God did not give him the Egyptian laws of morals or hygiene; he gave him something better. But he gave the laws to someone who had been trained in both the giving and the administration of law.

However, it was not enough that Moses had been trained as a prince in Egypt. He had to learn dependence on God and he had to lead Israel through the hard desert of Sinai. So for the next forty years Moses was exiled in the desert of Sinai. The arrogant young prince who took it on himself to

kill an Egyptian who was harming one of the children of
Israel, became, forty years later, the man who did not think
he could stand and argue Israel's case before Pharaoh
without God's help.

The protected prince had become a shepherd, the pro-
tector of his flock in the wild desert. He got to know the
ways of the desert, how to avoid its dangers and to stay
alive. Only then was he allowed to go back to Egypt and
lead God's people out.

David

David was another great leader of Israel, the first to establish his country as a major power, the first to extend its
boundaries and to subdue the fierce kingdoms around it.
But he did not spring into this position as Israel's soldier
king without long years of tough training, first of all as
Saul's military commander. His promising career was,
however, broken and he became an outlaw hunted by a
jealous king. He had to learn how to survive in the barren
mountains around Israel's border and, as Moses knew the
desert, so he knew Israel's borders. When he became king,
his outlaw band became his bodyguard, his outlaw captains, Joab and Asher, commanded his army and no one
held all their loyalties as David did. Together they went
back to the borders and put all Israel's enemies to flight.

But he had been trained for war and not for peace. It was
left to his son Solomon to be the great and wise administrator. God also told David that his temple could not be built
by a man of war, but that he must leave it to Solomon, the
man of peace.

Daniel

Half a millennium later a young Jewish prince was taken
captive. Jerusalem had been captured, the temple taken

and pillaged by a heathen king and all the future for which
he had been trained was in ruins. However he and four
other princes allowed themselves to be trained for the
service of the heathen king, though on condition that they
kept to the customs of their own God, ate only what he
allowed and worshipped him alone. Like Joseph, they
might well have given up, but, like Joseph, they worked
hard. Three of them found themselves in charge of pro-
vinces of Babylon and Daniel, like Joseph, became the first
ruler under the king. And before that king died, he had
acknowledged Daniel's God. So, even in captivity, God's
people were preserved.

Not only did Daniel serve under two Babylonian kings,
but when that empire was overthrown by the Medes and
the Persians, he served under both Darius the Mede and
Cyrus. It was not only his reputation as an administrator
which saved him, but it must have helped that he was not
identified as one of the Babylonian enemy. He was not at
Belshazzar's last feast – he had to be found and summoned
to it – because he was not one of them. When they perished,
he survived. He survived at the Persian court despite
jealousy and an attempt to use his faith to destroy him. But
when that failed, the Persian king too acknowledged the
God of Israel and his successor allowed the Jews to go back
to their own land and rebuild their temple and the walls of
Jerusalem.

Learning and doing

We all want to take short cuts, but there can be no short cuts
in our preparation for whatever job God has called us to do.
God's work is far too important for that. If we want to take
the gospel to the ends of the earth, we have to learn the
languages which they speak there. At Pentecost, at the very
foundation of the church, when there was a gathering in
Jerusalem of Jews and proselytes from many countries, the
Spirit gave the apostles languages they had not learnt in

order to speak to the Parthians, Medes, Elamites, visitors
from Rome, Cretans, Arabs and others in their own native
tongues. No doubt, in exceptional circumstances like those,
the Spirit might give the miraculous gift of languages again.
But we certainly should not rely on it!

Learning other languages is a long hard struggle and
there is really no way round it. Crash courses will give us
stilted baby-talk, a year's work may give the vocabulary of a
twelve year old. To preach the full gospel with passion and
eloquence takes a long time; but it certainly can be done. We
have an English friend who is the pastor of a large church in
Barcelona and our Spanish friends tell us that he preaches
without trace of an English accent.

The industrial democracies are 'knowledge societies'. So
many of our achievements come from fast-developing
knowledge. With every generation there is more to learn
and more to pass on. A higher and higher proportion of
young people have to go to university if they are to do the
jobs which our 'knowledge society' needs.

Learning is a hard and rigorous experience. It needs
discipline and endurance and it is understandable that
there is a reaction against this. There is an educational
school of thought which wants people to find themselves
and develop their natural talents. Of course there are more
imaginative ways of teaching than learning by rote, but
society needs doctors who know their anatomy, engineers
who can build safe structures, pilots who can do a blind
landing in bad weather and farmers who can deal with
blight.

On the other hand, learning can be too academic and we
may need more of a mixture of practical experience than
we have at the moment. Some countries do have extraordi-
narily long university courses and six or seven years in the
cloisters is too long before facing the real world. Young
people feel the need to contribute to society and they
should not be held back too long. Doing whets the appetite
for learning and mature students who have had a job before
university often tend to work better. An ounce of clinical

experience is worth several chapters of Gray's *Anatomy* and a few weeks on the night shift gives the young production engineer a feel for what improvements can and cannot be carried out on the shop floor.

It has been weightily argued that instead of sending graduates straight on to second degrees, they should come back later, when they have practical experience. The business schools have courses for the late twenties, which many in industry believe give much better results than immediate post-graduate courses. Business likes the combination of the practical and the academic that many first degree courses now offer as 'sandwich courses'. There are also church leaders who believe that the years in the artificial academic atmosphere of the theological college do a lot more harm than good and that it would be better to combine study with work in a church. Meantime most people in training have to go through the system as it is and keep in touch with real life through holiday jobs.

But we do not spend time on higher education just to get the specialist knowledge for which we can all see the need. It is also to teach us how to learn and how to think. No university can foresee the problems its students are going to have to face over the next half century. But it can give them the mental training and the imagination to find ways of dealing with the new problems when they arrive. Henry Ford said, 'History is bunk.' If historians teach their version of history as the final word, then their history may well be bunk. But an understanding of past human behaviour, as true as we can discover to what actually happened, is of enormous help to those of us who have to face totally new problems.

Those of us who listen to the South American advocates of 'liberation theology' wonder if they have ever read the history of the French Huguenots. The French Protestants justified violence in 'Vindiciae contra Tyrannos', took the sword, and were finally victorious. But, in the moment of victory, their civil leader, Henry of Navarre, went over to the other side. Ninety years later his grandson Louis

XIV finally revoked their charter of liberty and they were scattered across Europe.

Long-term learning

We have two examples from the New Testament of people who spent much time in study before they started their ministry.

Our Lord himself, truly God but also truly man and subject to our limitations, spent thirty years in training for his three-year ministry. By the age of twelve he was able to debate with the teachers in the temple. By the time his ministry started, he knew his Jewish scriptures thoroughly and was able to see and understand all the prophecies about himself. When he was filled with the Spirit after his baptism, he was able to apply God's law to his own perverse generation. He was able to explain what, at first, even his disciples could not see, that the Messiah was not sent to defeat the Romans and introduce an earthly Jewish kingdom, but to reconcile all men to their creator and to bring a spiritual kingdom which included the Gentiles too. His earthly ministry was very brief, but it founded the Christian church which 'turned the world upside down'.

Paul, the apostle to the Gentiles, the writer of so many of the New Testament letters and the chief exponent of Christian doctrine, spent a long time after his Damascus road conversion in preparation for this great ministry. He told the Galatians that he went immediately to Arabia and only three years later did he go to Jerusalem to meet the apostles (Gal 1:17,18). In the loneliness of the Arabian desert, that great mind, guided by the Spirit, worked out the implications of the fact that Jesus was indeed the long-prophesied Messiah, that his kingdom was a spiritual kingdom and that the good news of redemption was for all mankind. Paul, who had been Saul the legalist and Pharisee, had to work through the role of the law in a gospel which called for a response of simple faith. It all took time, even for Paul, who was a leading scholar taught by Gamaliel. And that scholarship too was God's preparation for him. He was steeped in the scriptures, but he was also a capable linguist and he knew the great writers of classical Greek literature. Many more than the three years in Arabia went into Paul's great task as apostle to the Gentiles.

Although God's decrees are unchanging and his promises certain, his immediate purpose is hidden and, as the hymn says, 'God moves in a mysterious way.' So we can never know just what God has in mind for each of us. The world can change greatly over a life span. When I was at university, Europe was in ruins after a terrible war and there was no such institution as the European Parliament of which I am now a member.

We must, of course, start out with a general aim, but after that we have to do as well as we can in whatever job we find ourselves. We have to trust to God that we are building experience for work to come. Like Moses, David, Joseph and Daniel, we will only gradually be able to see the relation between our training and our life's work – and maybe the pattern will not be visible in our lifetime. We may sow and others may reap long after we have gone.

The moral is that our time of training is never over. Everything we do is a training for the next job and every experience, especially the difficult ones, should add to our total of knowledge and wisdom. So we should always do every job as well as we possibly can and try to understand it and learn from it. The more we learn, the more God can use us.

5   Working time

Learn the fastest routine for recurring jobs

When you walk into a plant, you can usually tell whether the workers are being paid for what they produce or are paid by the hour. Those paid for what they produce do not want to be interrupted by conversation with a casual visitor. Those paid by the hour are happy to stop work for a chat. There is a swiftness of movement, deftness of hand and rhythm of work in those paid for what they actually produce. They have a system in their minds which they follow automatically, and they don't have to stop to think about what to do next.

There are arguments for and against paying workers for output only. At its worst it leads to the old sweatshops of the textile trade and at its best it needs strict quality control. But it shows how fast we can do routine jobs when our income depends on it.

When walking round a plant it's interesting to stop in the middle and count the proportion of people doing nothing. In an exceptionally well-run plant, everyone is busy. In a badly run plant, about half the people are standing round wondering what to do next or waiting for something to happen. The worst I ever saw was in a steel mill in Asia where, out of a hundred people in sight, only ten were actually working.

Some activities need a lot of thought, but recurring routine jobs need a fast drill which enables one to get through them as quickly as possible.

One of the strongest objections to the production line is

that it takes away from workers all control over the way
they do their job. The production line sets the pace, the
exact task for each worker and the method of work. The
worker is reduced to a mere part of the mechanism, taking
away all initiative and creativity. Where Christians have
any choice, they will want a job where they can take some
initiative.

American folklore is studded with stories of workers who
have found a better way of doing a job and have climbed off
the shop floor into management or ownership – like the
Reader's Digest story of the window-cleaner who doubled
his output by using both his hands! It is part of American
folklore that there has to be a better way. The folklore is
often used to promote the capitalistic 'opportunity society'.
But Christians try to find a better way of doing their job,
not so much to make money for themselves as to make the
best use of the time and talents God has given them. So
Christians who have routine jobs should look for work
which gives them some chance of doing it faster and better,
even if the boring production line job gives higher wages,
as it often does. And we should avoid jobs where there is a
war of attrition between management and labour on the
pace of the job, a war where labour solidarity compels the
Christian to spin out the work. It is better to find a job where
our labour is needed and to which we can give all our
talents and energy.

Of course Christians do not only use their talents for paid
work. Young mothers who feel burdened by household
chores have a special need to find a working method and
rhythm which takes less of their time and energy. Of course
babies don't always keep to the timetable, but that's all the
more reason for finding a fast routine for everything else,
for getting ahead while there is peace, so that muddle on
top of a crying child does not drive a mother to distraction.
All else being equal, labour-saving equipment, furniture,
food, clothes and decoration are better than those that take
time and trouble. And even when we can afford all that, we
need a method which avoids a lot of rushing round, puts

everything within easy reach, including the baby, and avoids our having to stop to think all the time about what to do next.

Learn to work effectively

One of Britain's top civil servants when Harold Macmillan was prime minister was a red-faced energetic man who used to eat up work. One of his colleagues said sadly, 'His trouble is that he will never accept that some work is beneath him.' He was so dedicated to his work that he tackled whatever was put in front of him. He died early of a heart attack.

The person at the bottom of the organisational pile has to do whatever is put in front of him, though even he can sometimes persuade his boss that there is a better way of doing it. I sometimes wonder how Joseph persuaded Potiphar to let him run his household or the governor of the prison to put him in charge there too. But as we take on more responsibility, we have to begin to decide how to run the job, what work to do ourselves and what to pass down the line. As machines are taking over routine work, more and more people are having to decide how to run their job.

The first priority is to get into a position to decide the priorities. So long as we are buried under our own in-tray, we will never be able to decide anything. Other people will be setting our priorities. The reaction of the energetic red-faced civil servant was to burn himself up on the work which came in. He simply dealt with everything that came with the same wholehearted zeal. But that is to treat our work as if it were no more than an implacable production line over which we have no control and that is not, in my view, a Christian attitude to work. Christians believe that mankind is made in the image of God the creator and that each of us has a creative instinct. It is that creative innovative instinct to make better and better use of the world's resources which dominates the distinctively Christian attitude to work.

After we have done a new job for a time, we begin to see what needs to be improved. Then we work out what action needs to be taken to make the improvements and gradually we build up a sense of the priorities for the job. We also develop a sense of the potential threats to the improvements we want to make and the need to deal with those threats also enters into our priorities.

We are now in the position to begin to edge our work away from the dominance of the in-tray and to establish our own priorities. Of course there will always be routine work. But, just as we learn a drill for recurring jobs, so we should try to find a system for routine work which enables us to control it and not to be controlled by it.

Once, when I wanted to change jobs, I went to see the chief executive of a very large and prosperous company and we got to talking about routine work. His view was that, whatever the level of the job, there was always a considerable amount of routine work to be done. But it seemed to me that he was glad that this was so and I didn't take the job. Later his company got into deep trouble over the health hazards of their major raw material. If he had been less interested in the routine work of a chief executive and given more thought to the major issue likely to face his industry, he would have saved his company.

When we have decided our overall priorities, we need to reschedule our daily work, relegating what can wait, delegating what others can do just as well and putting up front whatever has to be done to maintain priorities and to avoid threats and hazards. It's also a good idea to maintain a weekly schedule of priorities and to review them more fundamentally three or four times a year, when holidays give us a break from the immediate pressures.

Delegation of work does not come naturally. When we believe that we could do a job better ourselves, we tend to keep it to ourselves. It is far easier to see the job that is in front of us than to see the need for time to develop a better

system for all our work. When my father was twenty-six, he
bought a bus and started a route between his home town
and the nearest big city. His friends and family all pointed
out the amount of money he would save if he drove it
himself. He said that he wanted to be a transport operator,
not a bus driver and even though he only had one bus, he
wanted to spend his time building up a business and he
couldn't do that if he had to drive a bus every day. So he
hired a driver. He was right. There was fierce competition
for routes among scores of small operators and the only
survivors were those who were able to place enough buses
on the main routes to give reliability of service. Had he
spent his time driving the first bus, he would never have
survived.

It is a good rule of thumb that if anyone else is capable of
doing a job which comes our way, it should be delegated to
them. The only jobs we should aim to keep are those that no
one else in sight is capable of doing. We should reserve
solely for ourselves only those innovatory jobs which improve the level of the service we are trying to give. There is
nothing so cramping to progress as a boss who holds on to
every job himself. Not only can we stretch ourselves if we
delegate, we can stretch everyone else too and only this
process of stretching discovers those who can take on more
responsibility. There's always a soft spot in our hearts for
the boss who, however terrible he was to work for, gave us
our first big break. It gives great satisfaction to a boss to
watch the progress of the high fliers whom he was the first
to spot.

Where jobs seem to have equal priority, we should do
first the ones which will be needed first. It's a great temptation to put first the jobs which look interesting or easy.
We tend to leave the difficult jobs until later, telling ourselves that we should get rid of the easy ones and then we
will have time to concentrate on the difficult. Up to a point
that is right. An easy job is often quickly done and, once
done, there is no interruption from those who are waiting
for it. But we do not know how long a hard job will take and

therefore it is safer to parallel our order of work with the order in which the jobs will be needed. That avoids the scramble and panic of a last-minute rush. Above all, the keeping of work in sequence with deadlines for each job gives constant warning of the slippage of lead-time and gives enough time to catch up before it is too late.

Even though we set priorities, delegate as much work as we can and schedule our remaining work load, it is not easy to find the consecutive time needed to do really creative work. We should look at the pattern of our work and try to set aside the time of the day or week when we are most likely to be free from interruptions. We needn't leave it until our boss has gone on a round-the-world trip. If he comes in early, we should stay late and if he stays late, we should come in early. Or maybe we just put it to him that if he calls us every other minute, we do not have the time to do the job properly.

Sometimes we need a free week to sort it all out. I associate various summer holidays, when there was time to draw all the threads together, with major pieces of innovation in my work. But we must never get too far from the work face. Work done in some ivory tower is too remote from the constraints of real life. Constructive innovation comes best under the pressure of real events. The general cannot always be in the front line, but a general who is never in the front line will make the wrong decisions. So we shouldn't allow the inevitable constraints of real life to be an excuse for failure to find the time to produce the innovations which our work needs.

To work effectively we need to know our own strengths and weaknesses. There are those who are so full of energy that they never stop to think and there are those who are so lethargic that they need strong stimulation to do anything at all! There are those who bounce out of bed in the morning ready for anything and those who only get wound up as the day goes on. We need to know the kind of work discipline we need to counteract our natural weaknesses. There is no universal rule on the best way to work effectively.

We simply have to go by trial and error, finding our own particular metabolism and our own peak working times.

The American secretary of state, John Foster Dulles, was full of energy and it was said that he wrote all his speeches himself in the air on his way to foreign capitals. The foreign statesmen at the receiving end wished that he had written American foreign policy at home with more time for thought and advice. It is possible to do some work on journeys, but I very much doubt whether that is the best time for creative thought. I have developed a strong personal preference for going to sleep on the journey and doing the equivalent amount of work at a desk, preferably beforehand. It seems to me that the arguments for working en route are in the same category as those of the student's who doesn't get up in the morning because he works so much better after midnight. He shouldn't leave his work until after midnight and we should not leave ours until we get on the plane.

Eventually we all discover our best working rhythm and, like the athlete or the oarsman, the best way of pacing ourselves over the distance. But, like them, we do not discover our limits of achievement until we have really put them to the test.

Learn to work in a team

The lonely genius is rare. Most of us have to work in a team and a team is best for most kinds of work. Artists, sculptors and most writers do express their genius on their own. But the rest of us get the best results by combining our talents with those of others. Moses is the first great leader who has left us an account of how he did it. He records that shortly after he had led Israel out of Egypt, his father-in-law Jethro came to see him. He told him he was taking on far too much on his own and he couldn't possibly do it without help. Jethro said,

'Why do you alone sit as judge, while all those people stand round you from morning till evening? . . . you will only wear [yourself] out. The work is too heavy for you; you cannot handle it alone . . . select capable men from all the people – men who fear God, trustworthy men who hate dishonest gain – and appoint them as officials over thousands, hundreds, fifties and tens. Have them serve as judges for the people at all times, but have them bring every difficult case to you; the simple cases they can decide themselves. That will make your load lighter, because they will share it with you. If you do this and God so commands, you will be able to stand the strain, and all these people will go home satisfied' (Exod 18:14–23).

The record says, 'Moses listened to his father-in-law and did everything he said' (Exod 18:24).

The apostles were the team Jesus created to found the Christian church. They all seem to have had different characters – Peter and Andrew, the simple fishermen, Paul the Pharisee, with his learning, logic and languages, the loving John, to whom Jesus finally entrusted his mother, with his brother James, for both of whom their mother had great ambitions – yet they composed the group who were reported to have turned the world upside down with their teaching.

When individual churches were set up, they were to be governed by a group of elders, assisted by deacons. There seems too to have been a group of women deaconesses in each church.

None of this these illustrations takes away from the need for leadership. Moses was the undoubted leader of Israel and had to put down the rebellion of Korah (Num 16). In the council of Jerusalem (Acts 15), James seems to have been the acknowledged leader of the apostles and, though this is inferred rather than decreed, there seems to have been a leader among the church elders too.

Even the individual church is seen as an organic unity,

with each part of the body contributing its particular function, but each depending on all the other parts, as Paul points out to the Corinthians (1 Cor 12:12–27). The Christian faith is attacked as being too individualistic, compared with socialist collectivism. But the Christian church is a much more thorough collective than any trade union and it brings together much more diverse talents; it crosses the rigid lines of class and race, its demands for loyalty are far greater and its discipline is far more fundamental.

So Christians, above all people, should be able to work effectively in a team. Although it is said cynically that the best number of people on a committee is one, an effective group working together can be immeasurably more effective than one dictator. It is not just that a group can contribute far wider experience and knowledge, but the interaction of ideas between different people tackling the same problem can produce possibilities which one person on their own would never have thought of. There are few events more stimulating than a creative discussion between well-informed colleagues.

But personal ambition, arrogance, envy and sheer mischief can wreck all the potential good and enable the cynics to argue that discussion is a total waste of time. So, in any group work, the Christian, whatever his technical expertise, has a special contribution as a peacemaker. Working in a team needs mutual trust and mutual respect. Trust and respect take time to build. Paul found that the church which he had founded at Corinth had broken up into factions, each of which believed that it had the special gift and that its particular aspect of truth was the only one which was valid (1 Cor 1:10–17). Paul's first letter to them shows him as the peacemaker, pointing out that we do not all have the same gifts, that we must recognise the validity of other people's gifts and the contribution we all make to each other. We could well take that letter to the Corinthian church as our guide to any peacemaking which is needed in the group in which we work. Although Paul has some hard things to say, he is courteous, logical, patient and tries to show that, despite what has been said about him, he really does have no personal axe to grind, except that he founded the church and cares for it more than any of those who want to push him out.

Most people in a team have a contribution to make. The young turks despise the old sweats. But though the old sweats may not be as well-educated or as scientifically trained, it is a great mistake to ignore them. They have long years of experience and if something worries them, it is as well to listen. They may not be able to come up with the right answer or to be able to hold their own in argument, but it is as well to find the real reasons behind their unease. If, on the other hand, the young are on to something new, there is no point in dismissing them as 'just out of the egg'. The world does change and we need to be able to assimilate new knowledge into our work if we are to give the best service.

It is hard to put your finger on 'team spirit', but you recognise it when it is there and you feel the cold when it goes. During my first year in Cambridge, I rowed in the college eight under the president, John Garson, who could enthuse us all. I came off my bicycle and knocked myself out on the way to the river for the first of the May races. I arrived at the boathouse, still feeling dazed, just as the eight was being put in the water and asked John what I should do. He said, 'Jump in and row as hard as you can and you'll feel much better.' I didn't really believe him, but I felt I owed it to him and to the rest of the crew. I rowed badly, but he kept us going and we stayed 'head of the river'. The next year, we had two members of the university boat in our eight, one as president and one as stroke. They argued with each other all the time, morale was destroyed and we lost every race.

On a much more sophisticated level, the best boss I ever had was Lord Plowden, who created a team to run the British Aluminium Company after the fiercest takeover the City of London had ever seen. There were the old

executives of the British Aluminium Company, resentful at
having been taken over and a slightly uneasy Anglo-
American partnership, Reynolds-TI Aluminium, who had
taken charge. Then there were outsiders like myself whom
he had brought in. By a combination of courtesy, frankness,
firmness and fairness, not to mention a formidable mind
which all of us had to respect, he created a new team and
made us work together – but not before he had told us at an
early board meeting that if, in future, any member mentioned Reynolds, TI or the old British Aluminium Company
he would be asked to resign forthwith. No one doubted him
and from then on we all worked for the same company.

There is nothing which weakens a working group more
than rows. It drains emotional energy, it creates mistrust,
forms warring cliques and makes constructive work impossible. And if the working group is at the top of an
organisation, the whole organisation is weakened. I remember one very senior manager saying that he just didn't
seem to be able to help himself. He knew that what he said
did harm, but he couldn't keep his bitterness back. It was
not entirely his fault. He had been provoked for years by
irresponsible bosses and yet had loyally helped to keep the
team together; but he had now got to the very end of his
limits of tolerance.

The more complex our society and the more interdepen-
dent we become, the more it matters that people who work
together are able to respect and tolerate each other. There is
no official statistic of tolerance levels, but if there were, I
imagine it would show a steep decline.

One of the many management truths which I learnt
from the great American management consultant, Peter
Drucker, was that the best way to put a team together was
to concentrate on people's strengths and not their weaknesses. We all have weaknesses, things we cannot do. What is
important in a team is the contribution which each member
can make. All that matters in the end is the total contribution
which can be made by the total team. God gives the church
enough talents to do what he has asked us to do, so we have

absolutely no excuse for concentrating on people's weak-nesses. If we are part of a secular team, we have to make sure that we put together the talents that we need, or cut back our ambitions to what can be done by the team we have.

Learn how to buy time on the job

As people take on more responsibility, their time becomes more precious. A lot of people spend ten hours a week commuting from the country each day to work in a big city. Some even spend fifteen hours a week travelling from door to door. That doesn't include the time they spend in waiting for infrequent rail services. In relation to a forty hour week, that seems excessive. If we priced total travel time at the hourly cost of our time to our company or client, we would need to occupy a very junior job to make the savings of living so far from the centre worthwhile. In the old days the boss lived on top of the shop, his travel time was nil and he didn't have to stop in the middle of his business to dash off for a train.

There's a lot to be said for bosses living near their work quite apart from the amount of travel time. Maybe we would not have such dereliction in the inner cities if more bosses lived there. Or maybe a lot more workers could live in pleasant surroundings in a country town. There is also a lot to be said for the young professional and young execu-tive living near their work even if the economic equation is not so compelling. And socially, the habit of commuting produces one-class suburbs, which widens the gap between class and class and creates a divided society.

Cheap air fares with flights which cannot be changed or standby seats which may not be available for days on end, are for those whose time is cheap. While we had a house in London, we used to have calls from American students after each summer school in Austria. 'Hi,' they would say. 'Hi,' we would reply, 'where are you and what are you doing?' 'We're right here in London waiting for a standby seat, can we come to see you?' 'Sure,' we would say, 'have you got anywhere to stay?' 'Well actually no, the money's run out; can we sleep on your couch?' Our record overnight number sleeping in the house waiting for a standby flight was eighteen. At a Christian conference in Singapore, half the delegates were on standby flights. One university professor from Canada had to get back for a key examination. Day after day the flights to America left without her and she finally had to pay the full fare. Those of us who have to travel a lot by air could, on paper, save a fortune by travelling on cheap fixed-time flights, but we would spend a lot of our life waiting around in the wrong place and unable to be where we were needed.

There is also a great temptation to save money by doing work ourselves which could easily be done by paid assistants or to try to save money by taking on staff without adequate qualifications. We should always put our own added earning power on the other side of the equation and we would then find that it does not pay to do routine work ourselves when it could be done by assistants and that it does not pay to take on cheap assistants who are inadequate for the work. There is nothing which keeps older professionals more on their toes than a group of bright young professionals in the office. It is part of the policy, of pushing out the frontiers of knowledge and of application of knowledge.

Of course the money equation is just a method of calculation, a way of reminding us of the potential contribution, measured by what people are prepared to pay for the service. There are times when we will nevertheless give the service free. I spent eleven years of my life in three public service jobs, persuading industrial leaders with six-figure incomes to work for their country for nothing. And in the first two of those jobs, I had to persuade young industrialists that a temporary lower-paid job in the public service was also worthwhile because of the experience it gave them. And when we look at the kind of help which our minister may need in the church, we should only make the money calculation comparing the cost of his time saved with the cost of assistance gadgets if we pay him a very adequate stipend. But the principle is the same: we should find other people to do the work which does not have to be done by the minister and free him for work which only he can do.

Today there are all kinds of mechanical gadgets which save time. There are phones which re-dial numbers which are engaged, which store the most frequently used numbers, which let us know when the number has answered, which record messages and which will give us those messages if we phone in. We need to price our time to see what they save us and how much extra work they would enable us to do.

Even if the equation does not tell us to spend money to save time at our current earning power, it may still be worth making an investment if we have the money, because it gives us the time to increase our earning power. A student has no earning power but still has to decide how much time to spend in the vacation in studying and how much in earning. Lifetime earning will be affected by the class of degree and if extra time in studying will improve the class, then it is foolish to spend more than the absolute minimum time necessary in vacation jobs.

Learn to minimise sick time

The Christian believes that God has given us our bodies in trust, that they are not our own to do what we like with them, but that they are God's, to be used for his purposes and for whatever calling he has given us. So we should look after our health. It is a gift from God and we should not take it for granted. Of course disease can strike us all, but preventive medicine will minimise the risk. We now know much more than we did about the effect on our health of what we eat and drink, of exercise or lack of it, of tobacco and other drugs and of the strains we put on ourselves, like jet-lag. We have all kinds of preventatives and antidotes which we never used to have; so we have only ourselves to blame if we are incapacitated for our work by an illness which we might have prevented.

A very fine Christian worker went to Nigeria without the usual inoculations. He somehow seemed to feel that if God wanted him to visit Nigeria, God would look after him. He caught blackwater fever and died. Where God gives us the means of helping ourselves, he expects us to use them. We should not commit the sin of tempting God. I hate being laid low with flu and always take a flu injection in October. It's cheap and quick and has no side effects and, although it is not infallible, it seems to be generally effective. I cannot understand why more people do not save themselves a wasted feverish week – or more – by having the injection.

It is, of course, a great help to have taken up some sport when young. This gives us a feeling of physical fitness which sets a norm through life, so that we keep up some kind of exercise if only to retain the faint glow of the fitness we once knew. I can still remember the glow of pure health which I felt, sitting in the slender sculling boat on the ripples of the Cam, looking back along the long reach to Ditton Church. That glow will never come back, but it has kept me jogging for the last fifteen years so that it does not disappear entirely!

One great advantage of rowing at college is that the rigid training makes it almost impossible to combine with smoking. Hardly any of us smoked at a time when every office and eating place was thick with tobacco smoke. And if you don't smoke by twenty-one, it's much easier not to take up the habit. By now, most people who smoke are trying to stop it, so it is hardly necessary to add the customary health warning. I once sat on a council with the chairman of Britain's largest tobacco combine and, across the table, our most brilliant trade union leader, who was visibly dying of lung cancer. It is a vivid memory and even if I wanted to, I could never forget it.

The other blight of our age is alcoholism. It is trite but true that Christ, who in his first miracle turned the water into wine, does not prohibit the drinking of alcohol. I once saw Rev Jerry Falwell, in a TV service, say that we all know that the Bible prohibits the drinking of alcohol. We don't and it doesn't. The Bible is against excess, against drunkenness, against the princes who drink in the morning. It calls strong drink 'a mocker'. But nowhere in the Old Testament law or gospels or epistles does it prohibit alcohol.

On the other hand the Bible does encourage fasting, which is abstinence from what is good in itself in order that we may lead better Christian lives. It also encourages us not to do anything which would encourage other weaker Christians to sin. If, by our drinking moderately, we encourage others to drink too much or if our having drink in the house encourages our children to drink too young, then we should abstain.

My wife, Elizabeth, was brought up in a manse in an industrial town in South Wales where drink was the curse of the working classes. The families which were desperate, where there was not enough fuel for the fire, not enough money to clothe the children and not enough food to eat, were the homes where the father drank. As a result the church was temperance. At a dinner in Eaton Square in London, Elizabeth asked for an orange squash. The famous newspaper proprietor sitting next to her ordered the same with obvious relief. He told her he was an alcoholic and found it extremely difficult at such gatherings if he was the only one to order a soft drink.

Alcoholism is now the major industrial disease, the major reason for absenteeism among both managers and workers. It is also, of course, a major cause of break-up in the family and of violence, not just of loss of time at work. During the centuries when the Bible was written, most people were too poor to afford to drink too much. The princes might drink in the morning, but it was not possible for the poor and it was out of the question for teenagers. In our affluent society it is possible even for those who are out of work to drink too much. So the Christian has an especial responsibility for setting a standard. Alcoholism creeps up unawares. The alcoholic tries to go on for as long as possible before admitting it to himself and even longer before admitting it to anyone else. By then he is in the grip of the drug, which is exceptionally hard to shake off.

Yet there are many who seem to believe that it is not possible to get on in industry or in public life without social drinking. I claim no particular merit in not drinking alcohol. I don't like the stuff and, if that were not enough, I had to work for three alcoholics in succession and that would have put anyone off! But the only people who have ever expressed open amazement at my refusal of a hard drink have been communist officials from Eastern Europe, and that perhaps says more about communism than it does about my drinking habits. I've heard of many businessmen and politicians losing their jobs because they habitually had too much to drink. I've never heard of anyone losing a job because he was stone cold sober.

There's a final thought on tobacco and alcohol. Both are drugs. They are not in the same class as hard drugs, but it has been more difficult for those parents who smoke and drink to persuade their children that smoking cannabis is unnecessary and dangerous. It does no harm for Christians to show that we have no need for drugs of any kind.

Never retire

I used to work with a great Scotsman called Bill Strath. He was the son of a policeman from the Lowlands and had risen to the top in the British civil service and then transferred to a top job in industry. We were discussing a colleague who was reluctant to retire. Bill Strath couldn't understand it. 'I'll be off like a shot when my time comes,' was his response. He was a great golfer and countryman and only temporarily an industrialist and I could understand that he was living for the day. Just before his retirement he and his wife bought a cottage in a beautiful village in the Cotswolds. Then I heard that he had over-exerted himself in moving the furniture and had a heart attack. He recovered briefly and went back to the office; but he had another attack and died in a taxi on his way home.

Christians do not have to live for the day they retire. It's not just that we see our work on a higher level, as a calling of God, but that we do not look for our reward in this world. As Christians we live for the day when we will be with Christ. This is where we really part company with the worldly outlook. We have a relationship with God which the world cannot possibly understand and we know that while we are on this earth, that relationship with our Creator, which is man's ultimate and complete destiny, cannot be fulfilled. We do not want to go through the valley of death, to leave all those who are dear to us, but we know that, even there, God will be by our side.

In practical terms that means that the Christian does not feel the same need as the man of the world for a retirement paradise. We do not have to live for the cottage in the country or the condominium in the sunbelt. It is no tragedy for us if we die in the saddle. Many Christians agree with the old saint who said he would sooner wear out than rust out. We want to be useful right to the end.

The big corporations and government departments are retiring people earlier and earlier. This is partly because they are hierarchical organisations where the only possible directions are up or out. The world of politics manages it somewhat better. It has places for the elder statesmen who can keep in touch and give wise advice, but who is not expected to carry the executive load. The church, too, has its place for elders. So we should not feel that, because our corporation or department retires us, we should prune the roses or go golfing for the rest of our lives.

The great John Wesley went on travelling and preaching until he was over eighty. My wife's father, Dr Martyn Lloyd-Jones, preached his last sermon when he was eighty and only gave up because illness compelled him. But he went on working on manuscripts until he was too weak to do any more.

The average life expectation in the industrial democracies is well into the seventies and, for those who survive until sixty, life expectation is almost another twenty years. We should not make that quarter of our lifespan a time of planned obsolescence, when we live on our pension and contribute nothing. The church itself depends heavily on the time of those who do not have to go out to earn every day. So do our many voluntary organisations, in most of which Christians would feel they were doing a really worthwhile job. Local government, too, depends on those who do not need full pay for the time they give.

Robert Laidlaw, who had built up the Farmers Trading Company in New Zealand, found himself at the age of fifty-five in England, just as World War Two was breaking out. He was asked to become a lay chaplain to the armed services. He realised that he did not have to work to live any longer, that he could hand over his business to an able subordinate and he felt a very powerful duty to stay in Britain and do what he could in the war. So he accepted. He never went back to commerce. That chapter had closed. He spent the next twenty-five years in Christian service where his energy and imagination made an even greater impact than they had done in business.

Some of the busiest people I know are those who have retired. Instead of doing one job, they are doing half a dozen and instead of the routine of a well-organised office, they have to organise their own lives. But none of them would have it otherwise.

6 Talents for all

In one of our Lord's parables of the kingdom of heaven (Mt 25:14–30), he tells of the man going on a journey who entrusts his property to his servants. 'To one he gave five talents of money, to another two talents, and to another one talent, each according to his ability.' The man who had received five made five more before his master returned, the man with two made two more. Both were warmly commended, but the man with one had buried it and returned no more than he had been given. His master called him a 'wicked, lazy servant', ordered that the talent should be taken from him and given to those who had shown that they knew how to use it and that the worthless servant should be thrown out 'into the darkness, where there will be weeping and gnashing of teeth'.

There is another almost identical parable recorded in Luke's gospel (Lk 19:11–27). Where the Spirit wants to underline a part of God's word, we often find it repeated.

The lesson may seem harsh. But God's many gifts are given to us to be used. They are immensely valuable and we do not hold them for our benefit, but for the good of his kingdom. It is a terrible sin to waste the gifts which God has given us. It is to remove from the world a benefit which he has put there to help mankind. It is as if a tree decided not to bear fruit. Christ saw a barren fig-tree on his way in to Jerusalem on the day after his triumphal entry (Mt 21:18 –22). He said, 'May you never bear fruit again!' and immediately the tree withered. It may have been symbolic of his grief at the lack of faith of the Jewish leaders, for they

certainly never bore fruit again and the nation was scattered
not long after. But the moral is for all of us.

The parable of the talents also shows that though some
have more and some have less, everyone has some talent
and that those with more are expected to do more and those
with less are still expected to use what they have to the full.
Paul, when writing to the Corinthians, lists some of the
spiritual gifts. He says, 'In the church God has appointed
first of all apostles, second prophets, third teachers, then
workers of miracles, also those having gifts of healing,
those able to help others, those with gifts of administration,
and those speaking in different kinds of tongues' (1 Cor
12:28). Although it is clear that some of those gifts are more
spectacular than others and, in the case of the apostles, are
given greater authority, Paul made it clear that all are
necessary for the body of Christ, which is the church. He
points out that the body is not made up of one part but of
many, and that each part is vital to the whole. 'If one part
suffers, every part suffers with it' (1 Cor 12:26).

Let us look at these gifts.

Apostles and prophets

The apostles were witnesses of the resurrection of Christ.
That function of direct witness has passed and the revelation which Christ told them they would be given by the
Spirit is complete. Both Paul and John have made that quite
clear. But there is still an apostolic function in founding
churches. The great pioneer missionaries who set up
churches in Africa and Asia and, much earlier, the Roman
missionaries to northern Europe fulfilled that function.
There are a few still called to that great work and it would
still rank 'first of all' in any order of gifts.

There is still a prophetic ministry too. I would rank Billy
Graham as a prophet. He addresses a whole nation. He is
gripped by a vision of the future which he tries to make
people see in vivid and compelling language. It is on the

one hand, a vision of horror at where they are going and on the other a vision of heaven as he sees where they might go.

Listen to Isaiah, speaking to the heedless Jews:

The Lord says,
'The women of Zion are haughty,
walking along with outstretched necks,
flirting with their eyes,
tripping along with mincing steps,
with ornaments jingling on their ankles.
Therefore the Lord will bring sores on the heads of the
     women of Zion;
the Lord will make their scalps bald.

In that day the Lord will snatch away their finery:
the bangles and headbands and crescent necklaces,
the ear-rings and bracelets and veils,
the head-dresses and ankle chains and sashes,
the perfume bottles and charms,
the signet rings and nose rings,
the fine robes and the capes and cloaks,
the purses and mirrors, and the linen garments
and tiaras and shawls.

Instead of fragrance there will be a stench;
instead of a sash, a rope;
instead of well-dressed hair, baldness;
instead of fine clothing, sackcloth;
instead of beauty, branding. (Isa 3:16–24)

What a picture of a materialistic society and what vividly compelling contrasts! Yet a few verses further on, the prophet is showing the vision of redemption:

In that day the Branch of the Lord will be beautiful and glorious, and the fruit of the land will be the pride and glory of the survivors in Israel. Those who are left in Zion, who remain in Jerusalem, will be called holy . . . The Lord will wash away the filth of the women of Zion;

he will cleanse the bloodstains from Jerusalem by a spirit
of judgement and a spirit of fire. (Isa 4:2–4)

There are not many people who have the talent to make
God's warnings heard above the noisy, non-stop entertainment of today. But if those who have the gift neglect it, they
commit a crime against their own generation and against
the God who sent them. Often a prophet does not want to
speak, because prophets bring a message people do not
want to hear. But God gives them a burning fire, so that
they can hardly help but speak. As Jeremiah said, 'I am
ridiculed all day long; everyone mocks me . . . But if I say,
"I will not mention him or speak any more in his name," his
word is in my heart like a fire, a fire shut up in my bones. I
am weary of holding it in; indeed, I cannot' (Jer 20:7–9).

Teachers

If the gifts of founding churches and prophecy are rare, the
gift of teaching the truth is much more widely held. Indeed
every church needs someone with the gift. Yet there are
many churches where the Christians do not hear the whole
truth, because they have no one who both understands it
and who is also capable of communicating it. Those are the
churches which are filled with dangerous half-truths, the
seedbed of the errors which eventually destroy them.

There should be enough teachers to go round. But some
want to use their gift in another more profitable occupation.
Some do not have the time to study because the church
expects a pastor to do all the jobs which ought to be done by
volunteers. Some have their teaching gift crippled by going
to a seminary or college in which they have to spend all
their time on irrelevant subjects or even in combating the
errors of their teachers and they have no time left over to
study true Christian doctrine. And some churches will not
spend the money needed for a teaching ministry.

Christ said to Peter, 'Feed my lambs . . . feed my sheep'

(Jn 21:15,17). God's people need to be fed on the word of God. Where a really good teacher appears, the church fills. Where the teaching is inadequate, the church will go through the forms of teaching and worship, but they feel that there is something lacking, though they are not quite sure what. A good teacher makes God's word live, and not only makes people see the relevance of the word to their daily life but makes them see that only the word of God *is* relevant, that that alone answers the difficult questions which every other philosophy skates round.

The good teacher allows the word of God to dominate the exposition. It is not the teacher's own views supported by a scatter of proof texts. It is God himself speaking, the teacher explaining what is being said and applying it to the congregation. The divine teaching is given its full impact so that people feel that they are listening to God and not to the teacher.

A church which has had steady Bible exposition from a good teacher over the years and which understands the whole range of Christian teaching is not vulnerable to the tidal waves of opinion which sweep this way and then that, backwards and forwards across society. Whether they are lashed by Darwinism or Freudianism, fascism or communism, materialism or eroticism, spiritism or racism, existentialism or humanism, their teaching is founded on the rock and it does not fall. They are a firm point of reference in a bewildered society. And they are always there to point their generation to the saving truth of the Christian gospel. Those who have the gift of teaching have the duty to use it to the full.

Miracles, workers and healers

The gifts of being able to work miracles and being able to heal seem to be bracketed together by Paul in 1 Corinthians 12:28. Most recorded miracles are miracles of healing. The age of miracles is not over, but for the most part God uses

ordinary means of healing and the gift of healing is much
more common than the gifts of miracles. The miracles of the
Bible are usually a divine foreshortening of the ordinary
process which God has given. They are not the Cinderella
magic of the pumpkin turning into a coach and horses or of
the seven league boots of the fairy story. Water does turn
into wine through a long process. Corn and fish do seed
and produce more corn and fish and God who alone gives
life and health can give them back again. So we should not
think less of today's gifts of healing through medicine than
of the gift of miracles given to the apostles. They are both
means to the same end.

Peter, speaking in Cornelius's house, told them how
Jesus 'went around doing good and healing all who were
under the power of the devil, because God was with him'
(Acts 10:38). Jesus himself, in defending his healing of a
crippled woman on the sabbath, spoke of her as 'a daughter
of Abraham, whom Satan has kept bound for eighteen long
years' (Lk 13:16). So Jesus clearly saw his healing ministry
as the restoration of his own creation which had been
damaged by the powers of evil. He did not heal because he
wanted to give a sign, for he told many of those he healed to
go away and say nothing to anyone (e.g. Mk 5:43). But he
healed because, as a loving creator, he had to restore the
damage which had been done to his creation.

Those who have the gift of healing – doctors, nurses and
therapists of all kinds – are doing what Jesus himself did.
They are undoing the work of evil and restoring people to
the condition God meant them to have. The work of healing
has always been associated with the church, and where the
church has taken the gospel to new countries, the medical
missionary has been a part of the team. Where medicine has
been taken over by the state or secularised it is no less a
calling of God; but Christians in the profession should see
that no one ever lacks medical care because they cannot
afford it. If a society allows any part of its people to fall
below the threshold of medical care, then it is the job of the
church to step in once more to fill that need. And however

much medicine in some countries may have become commercialised, for the Christian the ability to heal and to save lives is still a gift and a calling of God.

Those able to help others

I am especially glad that Paul included the gift of 'those able to help others', because that is one of the most needed and least recognised gifts in the church. There are all kinds of ways in which people can help each other, but the sign of those with the gift is a real and committed interest in those around them. They are the people who know who everyone is, who notice if anyone is missing, who take the trouble to find out what is the matter and whether there is anything they can do about it. It is they whom people phone when there is a problem and they take time to listen and to give wise advice. They are the people who notice strangers in the church and talk to them and introduce them to other members, find out where they live and who lives near them. They make the coffee, do the flowers, count the offering, sit in the crèche, give their home for a house-group, ask those without a family back to Sunday lunch. They know the names of all the children and what their hobbies are and, last but not least, they visit the sick. There are many great stones which build a church, but this gift is the mortar which holds it together.

Administrators

The gift of administration is a cornerstone of any church. The bigger the church, the more the pastor needs members with a good business head to take charge of the building, the finance and the programme in order to release him for the spiritual care of the flock. Big churches, of course, must have administration, but there are those with this gift who have organised the erection of a building for a small and growing church which did not have its own building, have found the craftsmen from among the members, discovered sources of cheap material and begged and borrowed the needed equipment to put it up. I have had the honour of opening two small Cambridgeshire churches which owed their new building to two or three members with the gift of administration. Sometimes the pastor can have the gift himself. We know one pastor who has the reputation, not only of building up every church to which he moves, but of leaving them with a new church building too.

The local church might get along without much gift of administration – and many have to – but in the para-church organisation the gift is essential. Where hundreds of missionaries have to be recruited and trained, funds raised, currencies bought and sold, home leave fixed and home tours arranged, buildings bought and leased, then administrators of a high order are needed. We only have to read the horrendous stories of pioneer missionaries who went off in sailing ships, months away from home, with promises of support which never came. They sold their few possessions, moved into smaller rooms, ate less and borrowed until at last the dilatory committee back home managed to find time to send the funds they had promised. Billy Graham may be the prophet, but in these days of mass communications, the prophet has an organisational back-up. There is no doubt that if the Holy Spirit swept the country, no administrative backup would be needed to get the people to hear or to put the message over. But in the absence of the kind of revival which comes once a century, we have to reach our own generation in the kind of world we live in by using whatever means we can find.

Tongues speakers

It is a pity that the gift of tongues has become such a controversial part of the renewal movement; because as soon as someone speaks of tongues our first question is about which side he takes in that controversy. So let me not take issue on the subject of ecstatic utterances and whether they accompany laying on of hands. At Pentecost there is no doubt that the Spirit enabled the apostles to overcome the language barrier and that the gospel was understood by thousands in their own native languages. That language is still a barrier to the spreading of the gospel and the gift of languages is badly needed in the worldwide ministry of the church.

Of course there is much wider education now than there was two thousand years ago when either Latin or Greek was spoken by the educated minority in the Roman Empire. Today English, French and Spanish are common international languages, as are Mandarin Chinese in East and South East Asia and German in central Europe, both sides of the Iron Curtain. But even if we speak English, which is the most common second language, we can only communicate properly with a tiny proportion of the world's population.

Grammar and vocabulary are hard enough, but each language has a rich idiom and an ever-changing world of allusion, understood by those who are at home in the native lifestyle, popular literature and ways of thought, but almost totally incomprehensible to those who are not. Although the Nazi police spoke Dutch during the wartime occupation, the Dutch never had any difficulty in talking to each other in ways which the Gestapo could not follow. I work in a multinational parliament where there are nine official languages (we would have had ten, but not all the Irish speak Erse!) and seventy-two different simultaneous cross-translations. We insist that each interpreter interprets into their own native language because, however skilled, the foreign speaker can never find the range of vocabulary which the native has. And however 'correctly' we speak a foreign language, we really need a special gift to get on level terms with the native speaker. Those who have this gift are invaluable to the church and to the spread of the gospel and the gift of reducing new languages to writing and

translating the scriptures into them is of inestimable
worth.

Evangelists

Paul's list of spiritual gifts in 1 Corinthians 12:28 is not
complete. There are others mentioned elsewhere (Eph
4:11–13; Rom 12:6–8). There are, for instance, evangelists.
Leaving for the moment the place of the evangelist in the
church's public ministry, there is no doubt that some
people have a remarkable gift of personal evangelism.
Some of us don't, though it doesn't mean that we never
have the responsibility of helping an anxious soul. But it
tends to come on us as a great surprise to find that someone
actually wants to talk to us about our faith and an even
greater surprise to find that they are even more desperate to
find faith themselves. Somehow we can never believe that
the good God would ever send anyone like that in our
direction and really expect us to do something about it!
It happens to all of us, but some people seem to attract
them naturally and to help them to find faith even more
naturally.

I had a friend who was the secretary of a learned society
in London. If anyone was capable of answering hard questions about the Christian faith, he was. But people didn't go
to him for help; he told me that they went to his old mother.
I met her and I could see why. You would have been happy
to have told her anything and know that she would never
despise you. And she could ask you the most penetrating
question without your taking the least offence. She had the
kind of open-eyed look which would draw you out and
make you say more than you meant to say, admit what you
had never admitted to anyone before, even to your nearest
and dearest – especially to your nearest and dearest! Above
all you knew that she was as innocent as the driven snow
and you would have trusted her completely.

But you don't have to be a dear old lady to have this gift.

Becky Manley Pippert tells how it happened to her in her excellent book, *Out of the Saltshaker*. And Becky, whom we have known since she was just out of her teens, is no little old lady, but the sort of girl who used to attract men who were not at all anxious about their souls, though that didn't prevent her evangelising them while she fended them off. But she does have the same quality as the dear old lady; she is clearly so concerned about you that you couldn't possibly take offence. She is interested, she cares, she wants to know all about you, she shares her own hopes and fears and faith and leaves you with the question you cannot answer, which bothers you until you finally find faith. For example she was an enormous help to our youngest son and left him with the question, 'OK Johnnie, so who do you think Jesus Christ really was? Could he really have been some sort of nut? Was he simply telling lies all the time? Or was he actually who he thought he was: the Son of God?' About a month later, he finally decided that the answer he wouldn't allow himself to admit to was the only believable answer. Becky says that we don't know that we have this gift until we have tried to exercise it and that we should at least try to find out. And it's hard to argue with that.

The wise

There is a gift much thought of throughout history, but not much heard of today, the gift of wisdom. Today we are so flooded with knowledge that we have forgotten about wisdom. It is said that most scientists who have ever lived are still alive today; such is the exponential increase of science and scientists that it could well be true. But wisdom tends to come with age and anyone over thirty is out of date scientifically. Beyond thirty, the older we are, the less we know, so age is discounted. Ten-year-olds can use a computer when their fathers cannot.

It is only when we come to consider what the knowledge

is for that we see the need for wisdom. Science only asks 'How?' Wisdom asks 'Why?' Science tells us how to put a man on the moon. Wisdom asks why we do not use our resources to feed the starving. Science tells us how to target an intercontinental missile and, maybe, how to shoot one down in space. Wisdom asks where the arms race is likely to end. Albert Einstein was a wise scientist. When asked about the weapons of the next war, he said he didn't exactly know, but the weapons of the war after that would be stones.

Wisdom understands people. John said of Jesus, that he would not entrust himself to those who believed in him because of his miracles, 'for he knew all men. He did not need man's testimony about man, for he knew what was in a man' (Jn 2:24,25). We see his wisdom in the answers he gave to the hostile Jewish rulers. Time and again they thought of some hard question which would nail him for sure, put him in the wrong either with the Roman authorities or with the people, force him to make claims which would be the basis of a charge of blasphemy. Time and again he replied by exploiting their own contradictions. He asked them: Was John the Baptist from heaven or from men? If they said he was from heaven, then they would have to explain why they didn't follow him, if from men, they would have to explain themselves to the people, who believed that John was a prophet. Lamely they said, they didn't know (Lk 20:1–8). Or look at the way in which he deals with the woman at the well in Samaria (Jn 4). He will not let her escape with evasions and exposes her religious pretensions until finally she admits to living in sin and believes in him.

When God said to King Solomon, at the beginning of his reign, 'Ask for whatever you want me to give you,' Solomon said, 'Give me wisdom and knowledge, that I may lead this people, for who is able to govern this great people of yours?' (2 Chron 1:7,10).

Solomon's wisdom was based on his profound understanding of people. In the famous story of his judgement between the two women claiming the same baby, he proposed a solution which forced a protest from the true mother but satisfied the jealousy of the other woman (1 Kings 3:16–28). The book of Proverbs is full of wisdom which is as true today as it was three thousand years ago. Wisdom may be old, but it is not old-fashioned, for wisdom takes no notice of fashion. Our own days are full of folly, promoted by the most advanced means of communication and carried out with superb technical expertise. We need far more people with the gift of wisdom to see through life's follies and to suggest a better way.

Today the biggest folly of all is to believe that there is no God. Two psalms open with the words, 'The fool says in his heart, "There is no God"' (Ps 14; 53). There are far more fools in our materialistic society than there ever were three thousand years ago. Science may explain the design in nature, it cannot explain the designer. God's hand-writing all over his creation is as clear today as it was then and to refuse to recognise it is the height of folly. By contrast the writers of Psalms and Proverbs tell us that, 'The fear of God is the beginning of wisdom' (Ps 111:10; Prov 9:10).

If wisdom is the opposite of folly, then the wise will do the opposite of the fool. Proverbs tell us that the fool stirs up mischief for fun, will not be told where he is wrong, will not listen to his elders, will never learn, lets everyone know when he is angry and will not keep quiet. So the wise will try to calm down those who want to make mischief, will always check in case he is wrong, will listen to those with more experience than he has, will go on learning until his last day, will suppress his anger and will never say more than he ought.

Those skilled in the arts

Skill in the arts is another gift of God. When Moses gave his instructions for the making of the tabernacle, he said,

See, the Lord has chosen Bezalel son of Uri, the son of Hur, of the tribe of Judah, and he has filled him with the Spirit of God, with skill, ability and knowledge in all kinds of crafts – to make artistic designs . . . And he has given both him and Oholiab son of Ahisamach, of the tribe of Dan, the ability to teach others. He has filled them with skill to do all kinds of work as craftsmen, designers, embroiderers in blue, purple and scarlet yarn and fine linen, and weavers – all of them master craftsmen and designers. (Exod 35:30–35)

An old friend of ours, Quinlan Terry, who is an architect, won an award for a study in which he traced all classical design back to the tabernacle which these men built. All through the period of 'new brutalism' Quin Terry went on quietly designing and building in classical shapes until, as the public tired of 'new brutalism', he suddenly found himself the leader of a new classical school of architecture.

David was not only a brilliant general, but a poet whose psalms are read and sung to this day. No one has yet been able to better the expression of feeling which Psalm 19 gives us of the glory of God's creation, Psalm 23 of God's loving care and Psalm 51 of repentance. Indeed we are sometimes so carried away by the marvellous poetry that we forget its message. When David became king, he 'set apart some of the sons of Asaph, Heman and Jeduthun, for the ministry of prophesying, accompanied by harps, lyres and cymbals,' two hundred and eighty-eight altogether and under David's own ultimate direction (1 Chron 25:1). We are told that there will be music in heaven, so there is no doubt that music and poetry are divine gifts.

Secular talents

One of the great changes brought about by the Reformation was the abolition of the rigid distinction between secular and spiritual callings. The Christian church was seen once more as a priesthood of all believers in which all callings were given by God and the activities of all members of the church were significant in the sight of their Father. The physician was just as much called by God to heal the body as the pastor of the flock was called to heal the soul. The scientist was called to study the book of God's works, just as the teacher was called to study the book of God's word. The whole world was God's world. Dualism, which divided the world sharply into holy and unholy, sacred and profane, was a heresy.

The belief that each person has a gift from God has also led to a tremendous upsurge in the levels of attainment in all countries strongly affected by the Christian ethic. In the sixteenth and seventeenth centuries most people worked 'by the sweat of their brow' and few used their latent gifts. Today manual workers are in a minority. That would have amazed our ancestors, who had little doubt that manual workers were good for nothing better. They had no idea of the gifts which God had given to mankind and which died without ever having been developed.

People may have both secular and spiritual gifts. A pastor can also be a good businessman. An engineer can have the gift of evangelism. People like this have to decide which is the primary gift. Whichever it is, we have to develop it and not neglect it. Paul was able to make tents, but his over-whelming duty was as an apostle. He used his tent-making to give him financial independence so that no one could accuse him of preaching the gospel for money. Daniel was a prophet, but for most of his life his main job was the administration of the Babylonian and the Medo-Persian empires.

Those of us who have secular gifts sometimes wonder why God has not called us to preach or to build churches. The answer is that although the church is not of the world, it must be in it. Its members must do the same kind of jobs, carry the same responsibilities, work with the same kind of people, be under the same pressures as everyone else – and yet set Christian standards in what they do. The members of the church with a secular calling are the link between the church and the world. If they set standards which the world respects, the world will beat a path to the church to find out what it is all about.

But we must also remember that this is God's world and that all people are his creation, for whom he cares, whether they care for him or not. Just as Jesus healed the sick and fed the poor, just as he called for justice for all, so we must play our part in looking after the ordinary needs of our community and in its need for just government. So Christians are called to be doctors, farmers, engineers, scientists, teachers, lawyers, managers, officials, elected representatives – and to all the other jobs which are needed to create and distribute wealth and to organise and govern our complex societies. And because all of these are callings of God, we are therefore just as accountable to him for the use of his gifts as the one who has a divine calling to full-time work in the church.

There is a fundamental difference between a Christian calling and secular society's aim of 'self-fulfilment'. The Christian should always remember that the object of our calling is to serve others, it is not primarily to fulfil ourselves. The distinction matters when a conflict arises, for instance between our primary duties, such as those to our family, and our secular calling. A sick wife may hold back, for a time, the logical development of our profession. Small children may claim the whole time of a mother and her professional calling will wait. We have to decide to whom we have the prior duty of care, our wife or our customers, our children or our clients. There is usually a substitute to look after customers and clients and seldom a substitute for a husband or a mum.

7 Developing a talent – age 15 to 25

Starting at school

Fifteen is an awkward age. We were too old to let ourselves be guided and not old enough to guide ourselves. Yet it is at that age that most of us made the decisions which began to develop what talent we had. Miraculously most of us came through, aided by wise teachers and parents who helped us to discover what we were good at and gave us the vision and interest to work at it and get the grades which would take us on after school.

Some were less privileged. I remember a boy called Ray coming to our church. He had left school at sixteen and worked on a building site. He had been one of a cockney gang of 'mods' who had their own hairstyle and fashion in clothes. He was lean and sharp with clipped hair and piercing eyes. A little old lady he liked had asked him to go to an inner city mission hall and, greatly to his surprise, he had become a Christian. Shortly afterwards he came to our church in Westminster and was sent to my Bible class. He stayed for about four years, arguing fiercely, but always prepared to listen to others. He was prepared to listen when we told him that he should develop his talents. He went to night school, took the examinations he missed at school, and then went on to be a teacher and an outstanding evangelist and pastor. But the hard bit was the beginning. Once he passed the first examination he knew he had the talents to go further. The big step was going to night school when his friends were enjoying themselves.

The history of the Christian church is full of young people

like Ray. It was one of the ingredients of America's pioneer spirit. All the countries which really pulled themselves up by their bootstraps had this spirit. After the Reformation, few countries were so devoted to universal education as Scotland. Even the shepherd was educated. Scotland had few natural resources, but the products of its educational system were found all round the world. In nineteenth-century England, Samuel Smiles wrote *Self Help* to help people like Ray help themselves.

The Christian belief that everyone, whatever their apparent limitations, is called by God to use their talent leads to a high priority for universal education. Without universal education, talents which could be used will be buried. The church founded both universities and schools and endowed them for scholars who could not otherwise afford them. In most countries where the church took such direct action, the state now guarantees universal education up to university level. There is also an increasing effort to educate the disadvantaged and a great deal is done to see that those who would have been written off as uneducable are given the specialist skills to take them right up to the limit of their potential.

Those who find school hard are tempted to drop out. They are not always lazy. They may be having a hard time from their peers. They may have had a quarrel with a friend and feel lonely. They may feel that a teacher has been unjust. Or they may just feel that since there are no jobs for those who work hard, it is not worth the bother. This is a tough time for the family – and no families are exempt. Brothers and sisters will often get a hearing where parents will not, but parents who have a record of being unselfishly helpful will have a much better chance than those who think more of themselves than of their children. The state must do its best to have an educational system which balances the hard work of preparation for real jobs with the education and development of the whole person.

It is hard to strike just the right balance between vocational teaching and general education. Learning Latin to get

into Cambridge and learning history while I was there did
not teach me how to be an accountant. But I have no doubt
that Latin develops the power of analysis and thought and
that history has been of invaluable use both in public
service and in politics. It has been said that a nation which
does not know its past cannot guide its future. History may
not repeat itself, but the patterns of history certainly do.
God made sure that the Jews understood their history and
we should all understand ours. If we ignore or neglect the
past, we will have to fight its battles all over again.

But because the educational system does not have a
well-informed customer and is controlled very indirectly by
parents, pupils or public authority – and not at all by
potential employers – it does have the temptation to exalt
the academic over the practical. It does not like to think of
itself as a factory for turning out good mechanics. I like the
story of the industrialist who at last succeeded in persuading the local school to accept a visit to his plant. At the end
of the afternoon, the teacher turned to the pupils and said,
'Well now, you've seen it all – and if you don't get good
results, this is where you'll end up'!

Yet the industrial democracies, with ten times the average standard of living of the rest of the world, live on their
skill. They have to import most of their raw materials and
fuel and export products and services to pay for them. They
not only need the technical skill, they also need to continue
to set the pace in innovation and development. The limit to
pure learning is the number of trained practical men and
women who can provide the goods and services which
fund it. The great scientific revolution of the seventeenth
century was dependent on the change from academic to
practical science.

There is also an educational argument about 'élitism',
though it is hard to find anyone who will give that word an
exact definition. Over the centuries, societies depended on
an educated élite. Whatever happened to the rest of society,
the élite were given the best education they could get. The
Christian view is that all of society should be able to develop

their talents to the full, since that is a divine command to all of us. This concept is accepted in all democratic countries and in many others too. But humanism has begun to take equality out of its Christian context and to make it an end in itself. Christian teaching is that we have unequal talents, and whether we have few or many, they must be developed to the full. Some humanists seem to believe that it is our duty to equalise the natural talents, even if this means that society's educational resources have to neglect its best talents. Anything else seems to be labelled 'élitism'. It is, of course, much more fun to teach bright children and very tough to teach the backward and so there is a proper cause for some countervailing bias towards the less bright. But what we really need are the resources in an educational system to be able to stretch the talents across the range of ability.

Learning how to learn

But whatever the educational or economic system, individual Christians must do their best to develop their own talent. Perhaps the most important step in developing a talent is to learn how to learn.

It is only too easy to be a lazy learner. If you read a chapter of the Bible each day, shut the Bible when you have read the chapter and write down what was in the chapter and what you think it was meant to teach. Then open it again and check back to see how much you have left out. We all find that it is usually quite a lot. We may remember 70% of the content, but the chances are that we have simply read it at face value and we're really not too sure what it does teach. Then read, if you have it, a standard commentary of the chapter and ask yourself how many of those points you had thought about as you read the chapter.

When I led a young people's Bible class, I used to ask questions about the meaning of the passage we had read. When the workers in the vineyard, who had borne the heat and burden of the day complained that those who came later were paid the same, what did it mean? Was Christ teaching that all pay should be equal? When the owner said, 'Don't I have the right to do what I want with my own money?' (Mt 20:15) was that a defence of capitalism? If so, how did it fit the theme of equality? Someone would point out that it was talking of the kingdom of heaven, not our present economic systems and then we would take it to the next stage. What was the spiritual lesson? No one was clear. Then who was the landowner? It would eventually be agreed that that figure in most kingdom parables was Jehovah. So who were the early workers and who were the late workers? Again no one would know. So we would start from the reward. What reward was equal to all workers in the kingdom? Eventually we would agree that it must be redemption, salvation and eternal life. Who then were the early workers who complained that salvation was going on the same terms to later arrivals through Jehovah's generosity? Where else did we read Christ's words that 'the last will be first and the first will be last'? And why did this truth have to be concealed in a parable? Why could Christ not spell it out clearly? By the time we had finished, they had thought through the answer themselves and they were not likely to forget it.

The famous 'case-study' method, pioneered by the Harvard Business School, follows the same principle. They take a real-life study of a business problem and make the students work through it, finding out why the problem had arisen, looking at the various options open to the company, considering whether they had taken the right one and looking at the results. This makes the students ask questions and debate the options with each other and it fixes in their minds the management principles which the case-study illustrates.

In fact that method of teaching has an older history than Harvard. It is said to be the method by which the famous Greek philosopher Socrates taught his pupils and has been known ever since as the Socratic method. He was so successful as a teacher that he was accused of turning the minds of all of the youth of Athens and made to kill himself by drinking hemlock – but that should not discourage us!

A great many textbooks employ this method. They provide questions at the back of each chapter to make sure that we have a check on our grasp of what has been said. Some students read the questions first, because they find that it makes a dull chapter easier if they can read it looking for answers. Other students never study any subject without looking at the old examination questions first and answering them afterwards. It is as important to find out why we went wrong as it is to discover that we were wrong. A good teacher points out mistakes and the wrong assumptions which led to the mistakes, so that those mistakes, at least, are not made again. Lazy learners get the paper back, do not go through the mistakes and consequently they make them all over again.

It is easier to spot mistakes in the use of practical talents. A mistake in landing an aircraft can be felt. A wall either stands up straight or it doesn't. A German either understands your question or sends you to the Bahnhof when you want the U Bahn. And in science, the experiment comes out or it fails. So there is a strong case for trying out our learning. We can only read so much in books, but we must continually try out what we have learnt.

The process of learning one subject teaches us how to learn another. Once we have learnt one language, it is much easier to learn another. And before we learn the first foreign language, we really have to understand the construction of our own. If we don't understand the subjunctive in our own language, we will never understand it in any other.

It's rightly said that today people know more and more about less and less. We can see the results even in our churches, which take young men fresh from their long years in the cloisters of university and theological college, put them straight into church responsibilities and then wonder why it doesn't seem to work.

It is, of course, helpful if assistant ministers or curates know their Greek and Hebrew and can tell the Albigensian heresy from the Arian heresy. But they have frequently had no practice in settling quarrels, calming the neurotic, comforting the dying, controlling teenagers, forestalling the pushy or, most difficult of all, rebuking those whose open sin tars the whole church with hypocrisy. It is doubtful whether they have even been taught to preach, to make Christian truth stick in the mind, to hold the attention of bright and dull alike for twenty or thirty minutes. But, worst of all, too many acquire their Greek and Hebrew at the cost of being taught every heresy since the first-century Judaisers (though wrapped up as the product of the latest academic research) while being kept in ignorance of the major doctrines of the Christian faith. There is little wonder so many congregations are confused and so many churches are unable to hold their young people.

The dangers of specialisation are not confined to the clergy. The secularisation of our education, where schools and universities can no longer give a moral basis to teaching, places a heavy burden on the church, which it is only just beginning to pick up. We desperately need a moral basis to science because doctors are having to make moral decisions as their technology pushes them into life and death decisions, into deciding what is human and what is life and where life begins and ends.

An old friend of ours, who was an Oxford don, had a vision of a college where Christian professionals could come to study the moral implications of their work. We saw the need with him, but doubted whether anyone else did, and advised him to stick to teaching geography. But fortunately he ignored his cautious friends and founded Regent College, Vancouver, which has gone from strength to strength. There are now two similar colleges in the United States, as well as the London Institute for Contemporary Christianity, founded by John Stott, in St Peter's, Vere Street, London.

But that is not enough. Every church needs to train its young people in the moral implications of their secular career – and to start in time to help them choose the right career. Churches also need to be tougher in their duty of recognising spiritual gifts. It is all too easy to allow some distant training college or missionary society to accept responsibility for telling the ardent but inadequate youth that he will never make a preacher, the romantic but impatient girl that she does not have the patience to be a missionary. But the church knows its people better than strangers, and the result of church negligence is wasted lives and frustrated missions and churches. But when the church does locate real talent and an undoubted calling, it has the duty to its young members to help to find the training which best develops their talents.

Curiosity

Another great help in learning is curiosity. Language teachers insist that it is much easier to teach a language in the country where it is spoken. That is because the language is all around us and it arouses our curiosity. We see a sentence with one word we don't know: 'Strasbourg, le carrefour de l'Europe.' What is 'carrefour'? It turns out to be 'crossroads'. We think, 'Yes perhaps it *is* the crossroads of Europe', and the word sticks. On the German motorway, you see the sign 'Autobahn kreuz' and you quickly learn that that is the German for a motorway crossroads. Later a huge sign is hung from a bridge says, simply, 'STAU' and, once you have run into the tailback, you remember for ever after that a 'Stau' is a tailback. During our first visit to Rome together, my wife and I kept on seeing a sign with an arrow saying 'SENSO UNICO' and wondered where the place was which had so many signposts pointing to it. It turned out, of course, to be 'one way'. We have never forgotten that!

Persistence

To want to know is only half the battle. The other half is to
persist in finding out the answers. Diplomats learning the
language in the country of their posting read the papers,
noting down the words they don't know, the phrases
they've not yet come across. They read all the signs in the
shop windows and, above all, they keep trying out the
language on all the native speakers until they begin to get
the tone, the common usage, the appropriate phrases. We
ask the German teacher the appropriate phrase for a terribly
boring speech. She says, 'eine stinklangweilige Rede'. But a
German colleague tells us that the more effective word is
'stinknormal' and we reckon that, since he is a politician, he
should know.

One of the world's greatest comics, Charlie Chaplin, said
that genius is 10% inspiration and 90% perspiration. We
know that in acting and in sport, it is the persistent training
which makes it look so easy and natural. Genius needs that
rock-solid base of technical perfection on which to build.
We know from the stars of stage and sport that that takes
persistence. They are no exceptions, it takes persistence
everywhere, but in these days of 'instant' this and 'instant'
that, we are not in a persistent mood. If it doesn't give quick
returns, we are not inclined to wait. So, to persist in
developing our talent, we need to go against the stream.
We need, in that, as in so much else, to follow our own
Christian ideals and not the way of the world.

Practice

Words in a book can be dull, but learning by doing is much
more fun. There can be few professions which sound more
'stinknormal' to study than accountancy; but to practise as
you learn does make all the difference. Just to learn the
checks which an auditor must make is dull work. But to be
sent on a fraud investigation to find out why those checks

do not seem to have worked makes the whole dull subject live. I remember arriving in the small office of a company whose cashier had embezzled thousands of pounds, with which he had kept a mistress in Bognor Regis. There was a pretty dark-haired office girl whose eyes blazed with fury as she told me that he used to lecture her on going out to late dances. 'The hypocrite!' she said.

Examples remind you what to look for. This cashier had to keep two cashbooks. He never let anyone else write them up and never took a holiday – the old hands told me to watch for the cashier who never delegated and especially the one who never took a holiday. They also tell you what finally uncovers the fraud. After a new internal auditor sent a routine letter to all customers asking them to check the amount owing on 31 December, the cashier charged an expensive travelling rug to the firm's account and vanished without trace. I studied that part of auditing with a new zeal from then on and never failed an auditing exam.

Checking

Developing a talent thoroughly means more than learning. It means asking yourself questions about everything you have learnt, finding out the mistakes you make and going through them again and again so that you are sure that you will never make that one again.

An old friend of ours was called in as a management consultant to a New York hospital which was introducing computers as a tool of diagnosis. He had to compare the computer diagnosis with the unaided diagnosis of the consultants and said that his most interesting finding had nothing to do with computers. It was that the success rate of the average consultant was better than that of the most brilliant. The reason was that the average consultant was never quite sure that he was right and would always check back in time to catch a wrong diagnosis. The brilliant minds were overconfident; sometimes they were badly wrong and so their final performance was not so good.

Listening to the old hands

I learnt a great deal in my own profession by listening to the old hands. The managers from whom I learnt my craft had all been through the financial crash of 1931 when our great accountancy firm had been called in to discover why this tycoon had shot himself and that one had sailed for South America. It was from them that I learnt the mechanics of share-pushing and the method of building up go-go conglomerates, whose price-earnings ratios soared to the stratosphere – until the crash came and millions of small shareholders lost their savings.

Forty years on, by the early seventies, most people seemed to have forgotten those lessons, but the talk with the old hands over lunch and coffee stuck in my mind and I felt it my duty, from the public office I held then, to warn against the over-priced conglomerates. I was in turn attacked by those who were making money out of them, including many who themselves had a professional duty to protect the public.

When I went back to industry, I found myself as chief executive of a big construction company with extensive development and heavy property holdings. The boom had, by then, become a property boom as well. The big banks were lending to secondary banks, who were lending to property developers and no one was asking the question which I felt obliged to ask, 'Are there enough customers at the end of the day to pay the rents which were needed to justify these tremendous increases in price?' Those property companies foolish enough to overbuild went bankrupt, taking the secondary banks with them and threatening the whole banking system.

Cyril Kleinwort, a distinguished merchant banker, told me that he had been in New York in 1931 and that experience had enabled him to keep his head. Other Jewish merchant bankers had remembered their German experiences and none of the Jewish merchant banks had been touched. It was the younger generation who had been hurt. They had believed that there would never be a crash again and had not listened to the old hands.

We can learn from the old hands at every level. In any plant there is a store of folk wisdom. The young apprentice *has* to listen to it as I listened to the managers talking about the thirties' crash, but the bright young engineer would do well to listen too. The instinct of the old hand is an amalgam of years of experience and practice. It is not set out in the ordered method of the Harvard case-study, but it is no less authentic. It may not take into account the latest technology, but it takes into account years of experience of successive managements introducing the latest technology with mixed success. If the bright young engineer is to avoid falling flat on his face, he should listen, ask questions, analyse the answers and try to understand the vital message which *does* still apply to the plant and the product where he is developing his talent. In long experience in many walks of life, I have always found something vital in the folklore of the old hand.

8 Stretching a talent – age 25 to 35

Once we have developed our talent to the point where it can really be used, we will want to stretch it as much as we can, so that we give back to society far more than we ourselves have been given. We will want to bite off at least as much as we can chew and if we bite off more and find we can chew it after all, so much the better.

Finding a job which can stretch us

Our first priority will be to find a job which can stretch us. That's not as easy as it looks. There are all kinds of social pressures to take jobs which are safe and respectable, jobs of the kind which a girl would want her future husband to have, a mother would want her daughter to have. But those tend to be jobs in organisations which are so well established that no youngster is likely to be allowed any real responsibility for years. They will have titles and good salaries and cars and pensions and there will be 'career development programmes' and courses at staff training colleges, personnel officers to assure us that all is well and that real responsibility is coming soon, but they know and we soon find out that it will be ten years before we have a taste of it.

When the British business schools were set up in the 1960s, they were funded by that kind of established organisation and they thought that the graduates would come streaming back to them for jobs. But the business schools brought the young hopefuls together for the first

time and their network very quickly found out that the most
interesting jobs were not in the founder organisations. The
more adventurous set up businesses of their own. More
went into the financial services and business consultancy,
where they were given responsibility a lot faster. Of course
they had to work very hard to establish themselves, but that
was what they wanted. British graduates who had gone to
American business schools could hardly be persuaded to
come back again. I know, because I went there on a mission
to try to persuade them! But they too wanted responsibility
as fast as they could have it.

So we should not go for jobs where we will be waiting for
dead men's shoes, but for real jobs with a challenge. We
should not be bought by money, by safety or, especially in
our twenties, by pensions. We should not go into organisations where we will be cramped by bureaucracy. There are
posts for 'high fliers' in the public service, but there are also
jobs which are as cramped and limited as those in
bureaucratic private business.

On the other hand there are sharks around who have fine
stories with which to tempt the brightest talents and there
are plenty of hare-brained schemes which have no more
than a hundred to one chance. It is as wasteful to gamble
our experience as it is to gamble our money, and it is hard
for those who have gambled to shake off past associations
with foolish ventures.

In some businesses and professions, an overseas posting, where distance forces you to make up your own mind
without much assistance, can give real responsibility far
faster than a home posting, where you are always under the
supervision of a senior. I spent a lot of time in the construction industry and the young engineers on a site out in the
African bush or on a small Caribbean island very quickly
learnt the meaning of responsibility. If they could get a call
through to head office, it was a minor miracle; even a call to
the national capital was an achievement. The young agent
doing the preparatory housing for the Kariba dam on the
Zambeze had to hire every bush pilot and every old kite in

Africa to get the contract going before the roads were driven through (flights in and out were a hair-raising and un- forgettable experience); but he did a superb job. He would never have had the same chance at home.

Overseas postings also broaden the mind. I met a young European bank manager in Tokyo who discovered that it was part of his job as the father figure in the bank to be the official 'go-between' to arrange the marriages of the girls who worked there. When he first heard of this, he thought they couldn't be serious, but after enquiries from fellow bank managers, he realised that there was no escape.

In fast-moving technology, however, the home business is the one which is most up to date on the state of the art and those posted overseas can quickly become out of date. It all depends on where the new frontiers are in a particular industry and how important it is to our job to be immersed in all the technological discussions and debates.

Finding a demanding boss who can delegate

Being thrown in at the deep end a long way from help is one way of learning – we either sink or swim. Another way is to work for a very tough and demanding boss who is also prepared to delegate. Personnel consultants say that most people find that the biggest problem in their job is their boss. A good boss is like gold dust. I owe a great deal to the first boss I had after I left Price Waterhouse. He had just taken over a grocery distribution chain from his father, who had built it up, and he was determined that it should now have professional management. I replaced the clerk who had balanced the books and produced what management information there was. My boss also ordered a punched card machine – the mechanical predecessor of the computer – which was to give the management information on which professional business decisions could be made. He sent me off on a course to learn about the machine (on which I grounded my tenuous knowledge of what happens in the guts of the electronic computer at speeds a million times faster). He also sent me off to the annual conference of the British Institute of Management from which I quickly picked up some sketchy ideas and, more important, the ideals of professional management, which have remained with me ever since.

The grocery business on Tyneside had never seen anything like this idealistic pair before. The founder had known how to buy butter by taste and to persuade a customer to buy half a pound more than she had intended and he had had the instinct to put most of his shops in the right places, but he had never seen a print-out. The first print-outs showed a huge stock deficiency. My boss said, 'Either the machine or the system is wrong. If both are right, someone is taking it away in truckloads.' I then learnt the first lesson of the computer installation: 'Garbage in, garbage out.' But even when I got the input right, the stock deficiency was still there. I devised a new ordering system which gave control figures for each commodity leaving the warehouse. At that point a salesman visited my boss and took him to look in the window of a small shop in a back street, stocked with lines which the salesman only sold to us. It was kept by the mother-in-law of one of the truck drivers.

Not everyone can find a first boss like Grigor McClelland, who was later the first Director of the Manchester Business School – and even Grigor put his foot down when I hung French impressionist paintings in the warehouse canteen! But it is worth searching for a boss who can bear with you while you fight your way through in your first responsible job.

In the high-tech industries, young teams tend to get together, some coming from larger companies in which they have got to know the market and others coming from the research departments of the universities. That is certainly the pattern in the high-tech industries around Cambridge, England, and I believe that it was the original pattern in Cambridge, Mass. The key to the success of these teams is that they know the customers who may need the next generation of their product and they know where to find the scientists who can help them to put together the package the customer needs. They form the bridge between the research and the market which needs it. They usually subcontract the manufacturing and the management problems it brings and they can usually finance the business without much outside help.

Finding jobs for the unemployed

At the other end of the scale are the young unemployed who form partnerships to do work which no one in the regular labour market seems to want to do. Two months after leaving school, a group of friends who had not been able to find a job advertised for casual work such as simple repairs and decorations, clearing rubbish, tidying gardens, and so on. Despite unemployment, there was a shortage of labour for that kind of work, and prices were very high, so work came in quickly. Two of the fathers helped to organise the work to begin with, and very soon the whole group were fully employed and learnt how to organise themselves. For 'fathers', substitute 'church members' and maybe this is a way in which we could get some of our young unemployed church members into their first jobs.

Industry and commerce have, in the search for economies of scale, developed into bigger and bigger employment units and organised labour has responded by bargaining groups which can force wages up faster than the rise in output. Business has replied in both offices and plants by heavy capital investment which reduces the numbers of workers needed. Those with jobs are protected by 'no redundancy' agreements and corporations reduce the numbers by a slowdown in recruitment. This falls heavily on the young, who are least able, in a world of big employers, to find jobs on their own.

The Japanese solve the problem by paying the young

much lower wages, so that it pays corporations to recruit them, and by running a huge labour-intensive service industry where there are plenty of self-employed jobs. America has so far solved the problem by running a higher regular rate of unemployment and a much less rigidly unionised wage-bargaining system. In Hong Kong, real wages have responded very closely to the level of world demand and employment remains stable. In Europe the drop in demand fell first on immigrant workers, who were sent home to Yugoslavia and Turkey, causing a traffic jam all the way from Munich to Zagreb. But, with four million Turks remaining in the Federal Republic of Germany with close to citizen status, Europe now has a serious problem of youth unemployment which it has not yet solved. In Britain, the Asian community has solved it by buying up local grocery stores and newsagents and Asian families keep them open all hours and have even brought back home delivery to win customers back from the supermarkets. If churches are to urge the young Christian unemployed to use all the gifts God has given them, it may be that church members could use their collective ingenuity to help their young find their first job on which to stretch their talents.

Finding better ways to organise the job

After school and college, where all the authority figures were meant to serve the students, there is a culture shock in finding, in your first job, that the roles are reversed and that you are there to serve the authority figures. But when that has worn off the work begins to fall into a pattern and we begin to understand how it all hangs together. The third stage comes when we decide that we could organise it very much better ourselves. That is the dangerous stage for the Christian who wants to stretch his talents.

Of course we may well be right. Most work could be organised better; indeed most work could be organised very much better. But there are vested interests in the way it is done now. Jobs and income depend on it. Ambitions depend on it. Prestige depends on it. So 'the way things are' is jealously guarded. And why should anyone believe the latest arrival, even if he has read it all up in books?

Before we can influence other people's jobs, we have to have a reputation for doing our own job well. Before we can stretch our talent on other people's work, we have to stretch it on our own. The young doctor has to diagnose better, the young salesman has to produce more orders, the young pilot to make softer landings in bad weather, the young researcher to solve the problems which no one else has solved, the young production engineer to have less down time on the line and a better yield.

The first hurdle is often the most difficult, but it has to be crossed. And it can be done. Genius, as has already been said, is 10% inspiration and 90% perspiration. There was a patient who complained that his symptoms came on whenever he went to the pub to have a drink. The whole diagnosis and prescription centred around his consumption of alcohol; but nothing worked. Then the youngest member of the team went to look at the pub and found that it was up a steep flight of steps. The steps were the problem, not the drink – and the patient was cured.

Not only medical diagnosis is improved by going to have a look. The old man took the steps up to the pub for granted. It would never have occurred to him to tell the doctor they were there. A great many reports of problems never report the real cause of the problem, because the real problem is part of the furniture and so familiar that it is either overlooked or thought not to be worth mentioning because everyone must know about it. In a British export drive about two thousand companies set up shop-floor consultative committees to improve export production. One rather sceptical management thought that they might as well use the occasion to ask production workers for their ideas for reducing the down-time on one notorious machine. The workers gave their ideas, the management told them to try them out and the down time was dramatically reduced. The management said, 'Why didn't you tell us that before?' And the workers said, 'Because you never came to ask us before.'

The politician knows that there is no substitute for going to see and to listen. British politicians uniquely go door to door canvassing and very soon find out what is on people's minds. The public meeting attracts the politically motivated. But door to door canvassing is a complete cross-section of all citizens. By contrast the big organisation tends to distance itself through layers of hierarchy. Going round a small plant, the manager knows everyone, knows what their hobbies are, which club they support and what their husband or wife does. But in the big plant, the management seem to know no one, the work is compartmentalised and the atmosphere is icy.

It is not enough, in a large organisation, to know what to do. Getting it done depends on people and people have to trust you. Christ said that whoever wanted to lead had to be a servant, as he was (Mk 10:43). If those who work with us feel that we are there to help them, then they will trust us. If they feel that we are there to further our own career, to impose our bright ideas regardless of the consequence, then they will resist our advice and our ideas. In TV's *Dallas* we never see J.R. Ewing on the production line. If he treated his employees as he treats those with whom he wheels and deals, they would walk out on the spot.

Serving the public

If our boss trusts us because we have done a more than competent job and if those who work with us trust us because they know by experience that we serve the team interest and not our own and if the old hands trust us because we listen to them, then we may be able to make the breakthrough we have worked out. But there is still another group who can frustrate all our efforts and that is the group which pays all the bills, the customers. We all know of great new ideas which have been wrecked because the customer didn't like it. I once asked Arjay Miller, then president of Ford, why the much researched Edsel didn't sell. He said, 'I guess the customers didn't take to it.' Why did the rather specialist Mustang sell so well? 'They just liked it.' Why did the imported Volkswagen sell so well against the heavily advertised Fords? 'Word of mouth – folks told their friends they were a good buy.'

It is our job as a colleague to help the team. But it is our job as part of a business to serve the customer or client (or as a public servant to serve the public or as a public representative, to represent the public). So it is a very primary job to listen carefully to those whom we serve, to find out what it is, out of all the products or services which we can give them, that they really want. We will never make our breakthrough unless it gives the customer a better deal. Tip O'Neill, speaker of the US House of Representatives, told visiting members of the European Parliament that America would go on with two-yearly elections to the House because that kept the members near to the views of those who put them there and that was what political democracy was all about. The market economy is consumer democracy and, subject to the limitations which he imposes on himself as a political democrat, the consumer is sovereign in the market.

Keeping at it

Those barriers to the bright ideas with which we want to stretch our talents should not put us off. They do put a lot of people off. A great many young hopefuls with plenty of talent simply decide to opt for a quiet life, to play safe, keep their noses clean and enjoy their family and their leisure. As a result the world is a poorer place; the industrial democracies slow down and the Third World goes broke and its poorest starve. But no Christian should bury his talent. We do not multiply our talent so that we can fulfil ourselves, we multiply because it is a gift from God and he has given us a divine command to multiply it.

So the young civil engineer should try to cut the cost of an African hospital, the young designer should try to keep the quality with a less expensive specification, the young genetic engineer should try to cut the cost of food production, the young accountant should show where the production engineer can produce higher output for the same cost, the production engineer should try to improve the yield, the young marketing manager should try to find how he can meet the customer's specifications without insisting that the plant produces fifty different shades of white. Probably none of this can be done without the kind of breakthrough which goes wider than our responsibilities as laid down on the organisation chart, but the effort to get the agreement is what stretches our talents and that is an effort we must make.

9 Multiplying our talents – age 35 to 65

How far to climb the ladder

There comes a time, after we have managed to get our feet firmly on the rungs of the professional ladder, when we have to decide how hard we are going to climb. We have an income and a young family and we have worked hard to get where we are. We have to ask ourselves whether we really want to join the 'rat race' and work late every night. Do we really want to join the ranks of the 'Yuppies'? Is it fair on the family? And how about the church, where there will be pressure for us to take on extra responsibilities? Should we allow ambition to drive us as it drives our colleagues? Surely the Christian should not strive too hard for worldly success?

The drive for self-fulfilment not only keeps fathers and husbands away from home, it keeps mothers of young children out at work too. In the very proper Christian desire to protect the family, we react against the idea that our work is the only way of fulfilling our talents. We argue, rightly, that we must not make a god out of our professional gifts. They are not an end in themselves.

So there are strong pressures on us as Christians to settle for a quiet professional life and to immerse ourselves in our home, to be good partners and parents and to do our bit in the church. At work we stick to what is comfortably familiar and does not stretch us too much and we do not throw our weight around. There is a long history of such attitudes in the church, but our duties to family have to be balanced with our duties to our neighbours, our civic duty and our

professional duty of care to those we serve. Some family
obligations are overriding but we would not think much of
the doctor who put duty to a family dinner or a prayer
meeting before a life and death operation. Nor would
we think much of the doctor who did not keep up with the
latest drugs and was unable to give his patients the best
treatment.

Each of us has to decide for ourselves how to balance
these conflicting demands on our time and energies. No
two of us are the same, but there are some general rules.

First, we should resist, in this materialistic age, the power
of financial motivation. The ability to serve others must
rank far higher than the monthly pay cheque. Up to a point,
of course, money matters. We need to provide for our
families. But beyond that point we should choose service
rather than cash. We cannot buy the satisfaction given by a
worthwhile job. If we try, the money will turn to dust and
ashes.

Second, we need to give a very high priority to our
families. It is perfectly possible to take on a tough new job
and give the family all the time they need, but jobs which
take a young husband and father away for half the year are
destructive of family life. Jobs which we can organise
ourselves can be fitted around the family. Jobs where a boss
has us on call at almost any time can be very damaging to
the family. Mothers, with all the pressures of materialism,
not to mention women's liberation, and the quite proper
desire to use their professional talents to the full, are often
torn between children and job. Far more mothers go out to
work today than ever before. But there are far more dis-
orientated children too than ever there were before. The
child who can come home to a mother has an anchor in life.
But that's not all.

A mother who gives her children priority while they are
young, who uses all her talents to help them, multiplies
these talents more permanently than a mother who stays at
work. Any teacher knows the difference between a child
whose mother takes an active interest and the child whose

mother is too busy. When my own mother told me, 'Children grow up very quickly' I didn't believe her. But those years do pass quickly. They are only a part of our lives and mothers can re-engage first gradually and then fully in their professional world. Of course this is not always an easy transition, and those of us who believe in having a mother at home with small children have got to do our best to see that mothers can get back to work as and when the children are off their hands. The woman in Proverbs 31 is the pattern of the active wife and mother who supports her husband and children but who also has a vigorous business life on her own account.

There is no substitute for sons and daughters. What we give for a few vital years, they repay for the rest of our lives. In the secure family circle, uninhibited and irrepressible, bound together by the affection given and received in early years, the enthusiasm of the young brings new life, vigour and interest to the old. When they marry, the circle widens to sons and daughters-in-law, and then grandchildren open up a whole new world for the wider family. We can only pity the rich and successful who did not have that early relationship, whose children became like little strangers, and whose visits as they grow up are no more than formal courtesies.

The decisions on the family are open and obvious. It is harder to spot the spreading roots of ambition and to separate them from the healthy growth of professional competence. A young British lawyer and politician, F. E. Smith, said that the world was full of glittering prizes, and he ended his career as the Earl of Birkenhead and Lord Chancellor of England. But though he gained great prizes for himself, it is hard to remember any lasting improvement which he made for society. The apostle Paul gave up all the glittering prizes and said, 'It has always been my ambition to preach the gospel where Christ was not known, so that I would not be building on someone else's foundation' (Rom 15:20). He founded the first Christian churches in Europe and his work has lasted for two thousand years.

The Christian should sit lightly to society's ranking of one job against another. Too many people wear themselves out for highly rated posts, only to find that when they get there society's taste has changed. When I was young, anything in atomic energy was fashionable – not any more! Men spend their lives inching up the hierarchy of a famous corporation, and when at last they get to the top it is taken over by a corporate raider. Or the job we prized so highly turns out to be incredibly boring. I ran into a man I had last met as an ambitious young manager in a great accountancy firm. He became a senior partner and when I met him he had just retired. I asked him whether he had enjoyed it, and it was quite clear that he had not. The job was very prestigious but unfulfilling.

Life as a pioneer is far more fulfilling. America was not built up by presidents of the Chambers of Commerce, but by technical and commercial innovators. If we are to restore the rule of law in our destabilising societies, it will not be done by Lord Chancellors or the Supreme Court, but by those who can open the eyes of the public to the impending chaos.

Most of us will not be faced with such dramatic choices. But at each turn we must look hard at our motivation. Is it the public standing of the job? Or is it the opportunity that the job gives us to multiply our own creative talents to help our fellow men?

Multiplying spiritual talents

Where someone has a spiritual gift and the church is his profession, there is no conflict between profession and church. But even then there can be a deadening hand, masquerading as piety, which tells us not to push ourselves too far forward. Even on the foreign mission field, there are those who settle for the second best and, hiding behind their own culture, do not give themselves to the people they have come to help. There are churches at home whose leaders are not prepared to go out with their church members to reach the terrible needs of those who live around them. I vividly remember a cosy church whose elders point-blank refused a request to entertain African students.

Christ told his disciples, 'The harvest is plentiful, but the workers are few. Ask the Lord of the harvest therefore, to send out workers into his harvest field' (Mt 9:37,38). We must take our eyes off ourselves. It is not a question of our ambitions or our self-fulfilment. These are irrelevant. If the Yuppies want to develop their talents just in order to have a bigger house or two cars, that is because they have a limited materialistic vision of the use of their God-given talents. It should not obscure the vision God gives us as we look at the world around us and try to see how we can multiply our talents to help those who so desperately need them.

Multiplying professional talents

There is nothing new about human greed and ambition. The true professional ethic seems to have developed from the Christian duty of care and from the belief that we have a duty to multiply the talents God has given us and to improve the state of knowledge and practice in our profession. The professional learns from previous generations and from his own experience and then tries to pass on an improved state of knowledge and a state of the art to future generations.

The profession of medicine has made enormous advances. Millions of lives have been saved from early death and from suffering and disability. Engineering design has made great advances in safety. Electronics has taken a great deal of crushing routine out of work and has vastly expanded the capacity to manufacture and to design as well as making possible all kinds of products such as the medical scanner and all kinds of activities such as the blind landing of aircraft. Modern management has enabled us to double or treble our output within a generation and to cut drastically the raw material used in each manufactured product. The art of teaching languages has improved greatly in the last two generations, together with all kinds of communication. Even democratic politics advances as country after country finds that, despite the warnings of their previous autocratic rulers, they can give all their citizens a vote and see the country better governed.

The idea of development

There was a time when the very idea of development would have been thought to be self-evidently foolish. The medieval world looked back, not forward. They looked back beyond the Dark Ages to the stability of the Roman Empire, which they tried to recreate, to the science of Aristotle and the wisdom of the Greeks and, in the Renaissance, to the rebirth of the ancient literature and arts. It was not until the Reformation that there was a looking forward, an idea of the development of the God-given creation, the realisation of the power of those who belonged to God's kingdom on earth not only to pray, 'Your kingdom come, your will be done on earth as it is in heaven,' (Mt 6:10), but to use their God-given talents to put their prayer into action. The following centuries were ages of optimism and ages of development.

In the twentieth century the process went on because of its own momentum, but the intellectual basis was undermined by the widespread loss of Christian faith in all the countries which had been in the fore of development, especially in Western Europe and North America. The cross gave way to the flag and over fifty million people were killed in two terrible nationalistic wars. The intellectual climate became deeply pessimistic. Science, cut off from its Christian purpose of 'the relief of man's estate', became a frightening new and impersonal power and mankind lived under the new shadow of the nuclear holocaust. Only in the desperately needy Third World does the idea of development hold the centre of political purpose, but that is overshadowed by the gloomy, entangling forest of corruption and debt.

But Christians should not be put off by the spirit of the age. We should see why and how earlier generations of Christians worked out the doctrine of the kingdom, note the effect which it had on secular society and see what we can do in our own generation.

The Christian basis of the scientific method

Our times are dominated by the scientific method. According to Professor Sir Herbert Butterfield, the real breakthrough from the ancient and medieval way of looking at nature came in the seventeenth century among the Protestants of North-west Europe, especially the English, the Dutch and the French Protestants, the 'Huguenots'. There are now quite a number of books on this subject. The central figure seems to have been Sir Francis Bacon and his initiatives were institutionalised later in the Royal Society.

It was no accident that these men were Christians. Because they believed that God had given us the natural creation in trust 'for the relief of man's estate', they were strongly motivated to work together to unlock its secrets. The natural world created by a good God, however spoilt by the 'fall of man', would not be hostile, it would be benign. And, just as they believed in coming humbly to God's revelation in his word and not imposing on it their own philosophy, so they came to the book of God's works with the same humility, not imposing some Aristotelian system of science, but discovering, by practical experiment, the laws of nature. And being Christians, they also decided that the creature could only discover as much about the creator as the creator chose to reveal. The creator was the great primary cause and they would limit their work to secondary causes, to whatever could be handled, changed, measured, timed, described and classified. In this way they put a firm barrier between experimental science, which could come to hard and useful conclusions, and metaphysical speculation, which could not.

Because they were Christians, they not only believed that God was good, they also believed that he was a God of order, so his creation would also be orderly. They believed that as Adam had been told to classify the animals each in their kind, so could they. They believed in a God who gave reasons for his laws, who taught cause and effect. So they believed that nature would be rational, that it would have cause and effect, that these could be discovered and systematised. They believed God's promise that there would be no more great natural catastrophes which changed the natural laws, but that these would be stable until the end of time, so what they discovered would always be valid. And of course they believed in one God, so that there would be uniformity in the natural laws.

Pragmatic experimental science took over from intellectual dogma and the face of the world was changed. The real resources of the world were put to work as never before. The countries where the change took place were lifted from the poverty line, the child mortality rate fell, diseases were conquered, food became much more abundant and the population of the world expanded rapidly. Three hundred years later we take all this for granted. We believe, perversely, that science has proved that there is no God because Darwinian metaphysics has once more mixed unprovable speculation about origins with experimental science.

What drove the Baconians on was neither ambition nor greed, but the belief that they had been given a trust from God and that they had to strive to fulfil it. Despite our present enormous wealth, we are on the downward slope. We live on the result of their work, but we are steadily destroying it. The foundations of the scientific method were moral. It was not knowledge for the sake of knowledge, but knowledge as a trust to help present and future generations of mankind.

When the members of the US delegation of the European Parliament went to the Pentagon to discuss the Strategic Defence Initiative with the Secretary of Defence, the final argument for the programme was that no one should place a limit on knowledge. Yet there had been Americans who had pulled out of the 'Manhattan Project' for building the first atomic bomb, just because they still believed that knowledge *was* subject to moral limits. Knowledge can be used for good or evil, but it was given us to be used for good. Those who use it to destroy cannot reckon to escape the destructive forces they themselves have unleashed. The man in the white coat is now seen in a more sinister light as the possessor of power without responsibility. We need Christian scientists who will once more put science into a moral frame of reference so that it is clearly seen to be working for mankind and not against it.

Scientists have also done great damage by claiming too much. Without a Christian framework for science, the present generation is going back to a prescientific view of the world. The arts, where society wears its heart on its sleeve, reflect a world which is fragmented, hostile, disorderly, irrational and unstable. The popular press is full of horoscopes, and every kind of superstition forbidden in the Mosaic law is now practised in our 'scientific age'. But without public support, experimental science will die. If it is not put into a Christian framework, there will be pressure to imprison it in the framework of another ideology. Whatever does not fit that ideology will not be allowed and the free flow of ideas, which is the lifeblood of science, will dry up. There is enormous scope for those who have the talent to put science back again on its Christian foundations.

In the meantime there is great scope too for those who can meet the crying needs of our own generation, for instance the need to feed the starving world, not with expensively produced food from the West, but with food which can be produced cheaply without our heavy machinery and expensive inputs. There is also great scope for those who can simplify modern agricultural knowledge into easily learnt methods, usable by Third World farmers who have hardly changed their methods for generations. There is a vivid description in J. K. Galbraith's autobiography of the flood of agricultural scientists arriving in India when he was the US Ambassador. He complained that they were trying to teach the Indian farmer half a dozen new methods a year when all he could assimilate was one change every six years. (Galbraith reminded his readers that he was trained as an agricultural economist and spoke with authority!)

Improving the state of the art

Whatever the faults of the professions, they do give to each generation the objective of improving the state of the art, of handing on to their successors a substantial improvement in the body of applied knowledge which they inherited from those who taught them. The more modern professions such as aeronautical engineering and medicine have made huge strides in one generation; but even the more mundane professions such as civil and structural engineering have made great progress, enabling deep-sea oil production rigs to be sunk and seated on the sea bed.

My own very new profession of management has begun to establish a body of knowledge and has set up institutions to teach and improve it. A generation ago, management was *ad hoc* and instinctive and it was hard to persuade the average board of directors that it could ever be taught and learnt, let alone improved by professionals. My first letter to the London *Times* in the early 1960s was to support the setting up of the London and Manchester Business Schools. I was told by the *Financial Times* that they did not see that there could be any interest in a business page. But now business schools are an integral part of the business scene and there is not only a regular management page in the *Financial Times*, but a vast literature about management on both sides of the Atlantic.

The management teacher from whom I learnt most was Peter Drucker. He saw that management was not just about techniques, but that it was, above all, about people. He also saw that, while the older professions had the legitimacy of service to the community, the legitimacy of management was obscured. Like the professions, it had to serve the customer, but it also had legal obligations to the owners, who had the right of appointment, strong moral responsibilities to the employees, whose cumulative pay cheques gave them the biggest financial stake, and also to the community, which depended more and more on its wealth-creating capacity. Peter Drucker also recognised the potential tension between the standards of the professions and the pressures of the business on professional employees.

This problem of the legitimacy of the professional management has not yet been settled. Nationalisation has not settled it. Nor have worker shares. The German 'Mitbestimmung' has gone some way, but some say that it depends on the postwar structure of the German unions and others that the Germans can make any system work. And the corporate raider has badly undermined the legitimacy of ownership and made nonsense of the idea that the competence of professional management would be legitimacy enough. The lack of management legitimacy has destabilised the great productive machine of the industrial democracies. The workers feel free to bargain as hard as they can for whatever they can get and, since the managements of big companies know that the cost of a stoppage is thirty times the cost of a settlement, the rate of pay increases has run continuously ahead of the increase in output and the resulting inflation has discouraged saving, slowed growth and increased the rate of unemployment. The next generation of professional management will have to solve this problem. When they have produced a constitution which gives those who manage our industrial affairs the broad support of those who are affected by their decisions, we can recover the expansion we need to give jobs and hope to the unemployed, both old and young.

The breakthrough to democratic politics

Or let us look at politics. The Constitution of the United States of America was a breakthrough. Puritan thinking in the seventeenth century had created the intellectual climate for human equality, against which the eighteenth century had reacted. But the ideas were still there, even in Europe, but especially in the new world. Although the American Constitution set up a secular state so that religion could no longer be used to dominate the citizen as it had done for so long in Europe, the faith of the great majority of the founding fathers was Christian and it is the Christian view of the dignity of the individual which dominates the Constitution.

The American Constitution set the pace and Europe followed slowly. If other countries have followed the European democracies even more slowly, there is nevertheless a real belief among millions around the world that the dignity of the individual must be respected. One Latin American country after another has left dictatorship for democracy. Japan owes its democracy to America. Greece, Portugal and Spain have thrown over dictatorships to follow the European model of democracy. Britain set up dozens of democracies because that was what the colonies wanted, and though many have fallen back, the biggest democracy of all, India, has survived for forty years and shows every sign of continuing.

The world owes a great deal to the founding fathers who broke the mould. Yet, when you read the accounts of the making of the American Constitution, it was very tough going. There were tremendous arguments against ceding powers from the states to the new federation, against common external and internal policies such as setting up a federal bank. There were times when Mrs Madison and Mrs

Jefferson must have wished their husbands home! There were battles to be fought and overseas debts to be paid. The nation today rightly honours those who stuck to their principles and hammered out a constitution which had no precedent.

Those of us who serve in the first terms of the directly elected European Parliament have the same feeling that, though the job of creating a constitutional relationship between the twelve formerly warring nations may be tough, it is better to spend our time and energy in this great pioneering effort than to move in grooves worn smooth by a thousand years of custom. As we listen to Philip von Bismarck and Otto von Hapsburg debating in the city of Strasbourg which has changed sides five times in Franco-German wars, we realise the great strides which have been taken. As we run into fierce nationalistic resistance to the tiny but basic steps we still have to take to enable the European Community to function, we realise how much further we still have to go.

Where do we need the major breakthroughs today?

The great commission

As always, we must look first at the direct work of the Christian church, the 'great commission' to preach the Christian gospel. In some countries the gospel spreads like wildfire. In China active persecution seems to have produced the biggest increase in the Christian church since the days of the apostles; perhaps, because the population of China is so much greater than that of the Roman Empire, it is a very much bigger increase than that of the early church. In South East Asia, Africa and South America too, the church is growing fast. There seems to be expansion in Eastern Europe. In the great Indian subcontinent, Christianity faces resurgent Hinduism, which is gradually closing down the foreign missions. In the heartland of the Muslim faith, it is tiny and in its own heartlands, Western

Europe and North America, it has been in full retreat for years, swept aside by the tides of materialistic humanism and nationalism and latterly by a dangerous increase in superstition and the cults.

In some countries like Singapore, the enthusiastic young churches may need a period of relating their new-found faith to their secular lives, making sure that the pervading materialism does not swamp them. But in the West the church has to fight for its life. At least the churches are now composed of those who are there by conviction. Since the 'conversion' of Constantine, the church in the West has been overwhelmed by those who joined it because it was socially necessary to do so. No longer. Like Gideon's three hundred, they have been left alone by those who had no stomach for the fight. That makes for churches far nearer the New Testament model. The lights which still shine, shine brighter. There is a greater sense of purpose, a far greater awareness of the gulf between the world and the church and, as the destructive acid of humanistic material-ism eats into the pillars of society and the social restraints on greed and selfishness collapse, both the world and the church begin to see the need for the Christian gospel.

So these hard days are still good days to be alive, good days in which to serve the Christian church. Not all are called to the front line in the battle for the souls of our neighbours and for the soul of our nation, but for those who are, every talent they have is needed as they fight the good fight and tackle problems which have never been tackled since our countries were first converted from paganism.

The salt of the earth, the fight against corruption

The Christian church has also become acutely conscious of the values which we can no longer take for granted. Of course there was corruption in public and business life during the great and optimistic expansion of the last three hundred years. But there was also a widespread acceptance of Christian ethics as the final moral point of reference. It was the call to this moral standard by reformers which curbed corruption so that honest citizens could carry on their lives without being put in difficulty. Those standards are no longer accepted as a final point of reference. In a materialistic society the final point of reference is money. Humanism provides a flimsy barrier and custom a slightly stronger one. But once the miasma of corruption has undermined the trust which is necessary to the billions of transactions carried out every week in Western industrial society, the whole commercial basis of that society collapses.

Western companies who paid bribes in the great overseas construction boom of the 1970s because it was the 'custom of the country' were horrified to discover that their own engineering staff were being offered bribes by the local firms bidding for sub-contracts. They found that corruption does not stay in watertight compartments. It leaks all over the place and destroys trust as it goes. There is a great need in commerce and in government for those who have the talent of total trustworthiness and who can attract to them others who can also inspire trust. You do not have to have a PhD to handle great sums of money, but you do have to be trusted. Investors, employees, colleagues, customers and suppliers (not to mention the tax collector!) all need to trust those with whom they deal.

Work on a human scale

The organisation of work has been damaged not only by increasing distrust in society but by the creation of bigger and bigger units of work where those who make the decisions are further and further removed from those who carry them out. The armed forces regard the maximum workable unit as being about five hundred. But modern industrial plants can employ ten thousand. And modern corporations can employ over a hundred thousand. But in such huge units, work becomes totally impersonal and no one can identify with the enterprise. Wage bargaining becomes inflexible and corporations buy off trouble by paying more than the increase in productivity. Half of the economy, including most of the public sector, cannot be measured by productivity and yet it has to keep pace, so inflation is built into the whole system, governments can no longer manage the economy and millions of young people are thrown out of work.

There is, however, little doubt that organising work on a human scale is well worth the talents of those who want to take it on. The problems of industrial management make it a most unpopular profession and there is not nearly as much competition for jobs as there is in highly paid service industries. But the need for good front-line managers, who can get people to work as a team, is overwhelming. And the possibilities of organising work on a human scale have been transformed by the computer. Plants of over five hundred people are no longer necessary, but the transformation of industry from big impersonal production lines to small closely-knit teams will take all the time and talent the dedicated Christian can give: the rewards to society will, however, be spectacular.

Feeding the world's exploding population

The world population explosion makes economic food production one of the first priorities of the next generation. When my Parliamentary Committee asked the World Food Organisation in Rome whether the estimate of a 50% population increase in twenty-five years was a bit high, they said that it was the mean estimate. It might be smaller, but it might also be much greater. Any discussion with Indian or Chinese officials quickly turns to the food needs of their growing population. Both countries have managed, miraculously, to keep food production ahead of population growth; but the consumption per head is not very high as a walk along the streets of a city like Calcutta will quickly show. I have never seen so many thin people in my life as I did in Calcutta.

The technology is there. But we in the West use our knowledge to produce high-cost food and when we have a surplus, we dump it on to world markets, where it undercuts the Third World farmer and drives him off the land. He drifts into the shanty towns where he and his family have to be fed on imported grain, for which his government then has to pay out desperately needed hard currency.

What we need is research into cheaper methods of producing food, both in the West and in the developing countries. And we need patient and dedicated experts who will help the Third World countries to become more self-sufficient and also to find a saleable surplus which will help to fund the irrigation, the roads and the transport they need to grow and distribute their food.

Finding the right balance of economic power

The politicians have to take the economic balance of power more or less as they find it. Of course it can be nudged this way and that. Overweening economic power can be put down. Trade unions can be made more accountable to their members. National monopolies enter and leave public ownership. But it is not easy for a political party to go beyond this without a major change in public perceptions. I once spent an hour with the leader of one of our great political parties, putting forward some ideas for change. But there was no strong and cohesive public demand for the changes I was suggesting. It was clear that the changes had to be far more stringently thought out and then there had to be a major public debate, starting with the country's opinion formers, then picking up the many interests who would be served by the change and finally confronting the vested interests when the public mood was beginning to press for change.

Democracy has given the legitimacy which an educated

population demands from political power. A democratically elected government has the moral as well as the legal power to take whatever decisions are needed for the good of the state. Economic power does not have the same moral base. Share ownership is the legal base, but the shares controlling the corporations which employ millions of citizens are bought and sold like commodities by financial institutions whose only responsibility is to their depositors. Although the total wage bill in most companies is several times the amount of the dividend, the board of the company is accountable to the owners. The workers, like the customers and creditors, have to rely on their arm's-length legal rights.

There was a time when I hoped that professional management could claim legitimacy as the holders of *de facto* power, balancing the interests of owners with those of customers and workers. But the freewheeling buccaneers of the 1970s and 1980s, who ate long-established companies for breakfast, were the stuff of raw and unreformed capitalism and the tenure of professional management was visibly hanging by a thread.

The professionalism of management needs a corporate framework which gives a fair balance of economic power and accountability. The German system seems to come nearer to legitimacy than any other I have seen. But that depends on a trade union structure which gives a corporation only one trade union, so that its presence on the supervisory board of a company does not bring trade union rivalry into the final decision-making structure of the company.

Ten years ago British management offered to talk about a system in which there was an election of workers to the board by every employee in the company, regardless of union membership. We argued that if there were a strong trade union in the company, its nominees would be elected and if there were not, it did not deserve to have seats reserved on the board to the disadvantage of the majority who were not members. I put this to a trade union leader who was an old friend. He said we were afraid of democracy. I said that we were the democrats, the unions were the oligarchs. Neither side would give way and there was an impasse. But the lack of legitimacy is damaging. Without it, the *de facto* power in the main economic institutions of society is divided between the interests of the owners and the workers. Each has a blocking position and the whole of society is weaker. It is a problem which will have to be solved in the next generation and professional management will have to find some way forward. In the short term those at work can use their position to increase their real incomes, but at the expense of the unemployed and at a considerable risk to their own future. Yet, on his own, no worker can find a way out of the logic of the present balance of power. They need proposals which look after everyone's real interests.

Moral limits on the physical sciences

After the Chernobyl disaster there were few people in any country who did not believe that there should be moral limits on the development of science. There is a strongly growing belief that we are pressing too hard for short-term economic gains without knowing what long-term damage is likely. In 1984 the Greens arrived in the European Parliament and, though they have only twenty seats, they have exerted strong electoral pressure on the other political parties at both national and European level.

All political parties in the democracies now take very seriously the effects of pollution of all kinds and the only argument is where to balance the degree of control with the costs. In the rich countries the cost can be met. It is the poorer countries who are still tempted to take the considerable risks of pollution at the expense of the health of their populations and the future effect such pollution will inevitably have on their often already meagre agricultural resources. The need now is for science to turn from research on ways of increasing output to ways of achieving clean output at a cost which everyone can bear.

These are only some of the jobs in which a breakthrough will bring immense benefits to mankind. The Christian, however talented, cannot change the world. But, with God's help, he can show how the world can be changed by making the changes in his own small corner. It should be our aim to use our own thirty years of peak capacity to blaze a trail which others can follow.

10   Why should we give?

We owe it to God, who has given us life and salvation

When the apostle Paul was encouraging the Corinthian church to give, he told them, 'you know the grace of our Lord Jesus Christ, that though he was rich, yet for your sakes he became poor, so that you through his poverty might become rich' (2 Cor 8:9). 'Grace' means 'undeserved gift'. He was holy, yet he bore the full punishment of all those who had sinned against their maker. He came from a glory which we cannot imagine to live in the moral squalor of mankind. He gave up the worship which was his due to be hated and reviled. He left his home in heaven to live on whatever hospitality he could find. 'He was rich and yet for our sakes he became poor, so that we, through his poverty might become rich.'

So we should give, first of all, because of the example of Christ, whose followers we are. We can never give as he gave. He had everything and he gave it all. Even as a man, he gave his physical strength to the limit. He rose before dawn to pray to his Father. The crowds pressed round him all day. He walked the hot and dusty roads from Galilee to Jerusalem and back and his family thought he was beside himself. No one has ever given themselves as he did. He had no money, no place of his own, no means of transport, no security, no peace and, in the end, no friends. On the cross, bearing the sins of the world, even the Father had to leave him and he gave the great 'cry of dereliction', 'My God, my God, why have you forsaken me?' (Mt 27:46). But he never complained. He gave himself willingly, knowing that he was doing it because of his love for us.

This is not the place to go into the arguments of those who want to diminish Christ's gift, who say that he was not God, that it is not his gift but our own good works which save us, that despite our rebellion against our creator he owes us our pardon. It is enough to say that, for those of us who are Christians, Christ is entitled to demand everything from us and to tell us, as he told the rich young ruler, 'Go, sell everything you have and give to the poor' (Mk 10:21).

In our urbanised society, we tend to take all that we have for granted. A friend of ours has a small farm in the west of England, where she takes children from the concrete jungle of inner London for a few weeks at a time. They are amazed to see milk coming from the udder of a cow. When asked, they say that they always thought it came from cartons in the supermarket. Ours is a society in which poor as well as rich lose touch with reality. For those in other generations who lived on the borderline of starvation, the harvest thanksgiving service was a real prayer of thanks. But our generation believes that it is something called science which makes sure that we always have enough to eat and that the problem in both Europe and America is what to do with the surplus.

More primitive societies are nearer to reality. They experience all the hazards of life, know the results of drought, disease and pests and they are grateful when the earth produces its fruit. They still see the miracle in the growth of the tiny seeds into a full harvest which feeds the village, the wonder of the reproduction of animals and the steady growth of the kids and lambs into goats and sheep which can feed and clothe them. They do not take it all for granted as we do. They also have a primitive sense of gratitude to an unknown deity and a fear that if they offend, the crop and flocks may fail. Just because our scientists have begun to discover the mechanisms of the creator's design, we think that that explains everything. But to understand the design is not the same as understanding the designer. And the more we understand of the highly complex and finely balanced ecological system within which we are able to live, the less we should take our lives for granted.

God has promised that, 'As long as the earth endures, seedtime and harvest, cold and heat, summer and winter, day and night will never cease' (Gen 8:22). Christians believe that the system is stable because of this promise. But the more we know, the more we realise that a fractional difference in temperature one way or the other could bring ecological disaster, and that life on this planet is on a knife edge and is totally dependent on forces outside human control.

The Christian message is that the bounty of nature is given us by a good God for our enjoyment. The sun and the stars, the lakes and the rivers, the trees and the flowers, the fish, the fruit and the grain, the birds and the animals, the iron ore and the coal, the silver and the gold are all intended for the human family which God made. His original habitat for man was a garden, which was spoilt by man's rebellion. Then nature became 'red in tooth and claw' and the job of looking after it became a burden; further rebellions brought a second great natural catastrophe, but after that God gave the survivors the promise of stability – 'while the earth remains'. But despite the two great natural catastrophes, we live in a world which is beautiful and wonderful and still full of the riches which God has given us. Indeed it is only as we have developed the natural sciences that we realise the full extent of the world's riches. They are enough to clothe and feed upwards of four thousand million people – numbers which even a hundred years ago would have seemed incredible. If we can conserve the topsoil and find the money for irrigation, the ecological system will, within our lifetimes, be looking after six thousand million.

Christians believe that all this wealth comes from God. We cannot, as in the Garden of Eden, simply pick it off trees. We have to work 'by the sweat of our brow'. But nature itself and the health and strength to work for the fruits of nature are the gift of God. So are wives, children, intellect, art, music, inventiveness and language. Man may develop the gifts, but they are all given to us by a good God and we forget that at our peril. As the patriarch Job said, 'The Lord gave and the Lord has taken away' (Job 1:21). Jesus told the story of the rich man who could think of nothing but his riches and of how to build even greater barns to hold them, but God said to him, 'You fool! This very night your life will be demanded from you' (Lk 12:20). We know in our heads that we cannot take our riches with us, but we still behave as if we will have them for ever.

Another of our Lord's parables is about the unjust steward who was forgiven a huge debt which he owed to his lord, but who then went out and threatened all his own debtors that he would act against them if they did not pay up at once. When his lord found out about this, he was outraged at the steward's ingratitude and threw him out (Mt 18:21–35). That teaches us first of all that we, who have been forgiven all our sins, must forgive those who have committed offences against us. But it also teaches that since God has given us so much, we must show the same generosity. I remember once grudging the time which my wife was spending with an old lady who had a depressive husband. My wife said, 'She has nothing and you have everything. All she wants is some of my time and you have no right to grudge it to her.' I felt terrible and I've tried never again to grudge the time she spends in giving help and sympathy to those who need it.

There is so much need in the world

The world is full of people who need our help. Of course the need is so overwhelming and the amount we can give is so small that our contribution hardly seems worthwhile. So we tend to respond only to spectacular disasters and to leave the chronic needs to look after themselves. But we should look the needs around us in the face and decide where our help would be of most use.

The problems of population growth, for instance, are enormous, but they are not insoluble. But in certain places a drop in the rainfall brings death and disaster. As the trees are cut down for firewood, the soil blows away and the desert spreads. Soil conservation and irrigation cannot keep up. There are those who think that living the simple lifestyle in San Francisco is enough to irrigate the Sahel. And there are those in Europe who think that the need can be met by dumping surplus grain. But what is needed above all is a huge infusion of hard cash to irrigate infertile land and make it bear crops.

The American Pro-life campaign decided that it was not enough to protest against abortion, they had to show that there was an alternative. So they set up an advisory service for girls who were under pressure to have an abortion, first to give them someone to whom they could talk in confidence and then, if they wanted to bear the baby, to help them through the pregnancy and with the child when it arrived. The funds devoted to this counselling and care service showed that the Pro-life campaign was prepared to back words with time and cash and that it was not just against abortion, but in favour of doing all that could be done by good neighbours to preserve life. There was a real need and they met it.

Another group in desperate need of help are the drug addicts, callously exploited by the naked greed of the merchants and pushers. Once hooked, they are not easy to help, but society must not write them off. They need very specialised care and supervision if they are to have a chance of returning to normal life, and we should see that what we have not been able to prevent, we should do our best to cure. Many who are hooked are just curious children who have no conception of the power of the drug or of its lethal effect. We have a duty to give them a road back to sanity.

Christ healed the sick and the church has followed its master. Medicine has always been an arm of missionary work. Hudson Taylor, founder of the China Inland Mission, was a doctor and the story of his mission is alive with the work of healing. Where there is a mission station, there is usually a clinic or a hospital. The industrial democracies have made great advances in medicine which the Third World still lacks. But, where they can find the money, Third World governments are doing their best to follow. I remember going into the newly opened children's ward in an African country and seeing them receive proper treatment for the first time in the history of their district. No longer need they be maimed or crippled for life, no longer need they die before they are only a few years old.

Financing the church and its mission

The Christian church needs our money too. The story of the early church tells us that money was raised for the maintenance of the local teaching elders and the evangelists who travelled from place to place to preach the gospel, and for the care of the needy in their own church as well as the churches in other countries which had been hit by disaster.

Christ himself, before he was taken from his disciples, gave them the great commission to go out into all the world to preach the gospel to every nation (Mt 28:18–20). It took them some time before the real extent of this commission dawned on them. Indeed they only started when they were driven out by persecution, first to Samaria and then beyond. It was only when a Roman centurion, Cornelius, became a Christian and unmistakably received the Holy Spirit that they began to face the reality of the command to go to the Gentiles. But by the time that Paul was writing to the churches in Asia, Greece and Rome, it was clear that there was a divinely inspired ministry which had to be financed. But the very fact that Paul had to make this point to them shows how easy it was, even then, to assume that someone else was supporting the evangelists.

The gospel spread in the first five hundred years of the church eastwards as far as India and westwards throughout the Roman Empire. As the empire collapsed, the church took the message to the tribes of Central and Northern Europe, until all Europe was nominally Christian. With the spread of Islam there was a setback. Gradually the church itself became rich and corrupt. Then came the Reformation and the discovery of America, Asia and Africa, and slowly the spread of the gospel began again, but it did not take off until the nineteenth century when thousands of young men and women poured out of the churches of the old Christian countries to Asia, Africa and South America. There was an 'open century' from the mid-nineteenth to the mid-twentieth century. But although many countries are now closed to foreign missionaries, enough are still open to absorb all who will go. And not all missionaries today are white. Strong African churches, for example, send missionaries to neighbouring countries where the church is weak. But all of them have one thing in common. To found new churches, they need support from the old ones.

Hudson Taylor inspired the nineteenth-century church with the need of the millions in China who had never heard the Christian gospel. Since then the population of the world has doubled and in the last twenty-five years the graph has risen almost vertically. Within a generation our world could perhaps contain the majority of adults who have ever lived. The great increase in population is coming in Asia, which is the continent least covered by Christian churches. So there is a greater need for spreading the gospel than there has ever been before. If we believe as Christ taught us that 'no man comes to the Father except by me' then the Christian gospel is the only way to reconcile mankind to its maker and there is a need which we simply must meet.

The New Testament also teaches us to take care of those in need within the church. Brothers and sisters in the Christian faith have a firm duty to care for each other. The apostolic church was told to care for widows who had no family left to care for them, and to help the mother church at Jerusalem, where there was a famine. The rich have to care for the poor in the church, all those who have plenty for all those who do not have enough and rich churches for poor churches, so that the world can see the Christian precept of mutual love demonstrated in practice.

It is this spirit of love which should drive us on and which should empty our pockets when we see a need which we can help to meet. The world believes that people put their money where their hearts are. If rich Christians show no evident care for the poor in their own church, the world will see no difference between the church and our materialistic society. Jesus said, 'By this shall all men know that you are my disciples, that you love one another' (Jn 13:35). Love is practical. It is more concerned for others than for ourselves. It is quick to see a need and to try to find a way to meet it. It checks back to find whether the help was enough, whether the need has really been met. And love does not humiliate the recipients. It does what can be done with the least possible fuss, leaving the least possible sense of obligation. Read the ends of Paul's letters. He knows everyone by name, knows what each one has done for the church, gives each the same dignity. He shows the fine pastor's care and each one of us should show the same loving care for Christ's body, which is the church.

Eternal reward

There is one final reason for giving. It is that Christ has promised eternal reward. For some reason our generation does not seem to like this idea of a divine *quid pro quo*. We say that if something is right, it is its own reward and that reward introduces a mercenary element into what should be a spiritual relationship. Certainly it goes against the egalitarian spirit of the age. We do not like the idea that there should be any differences between the saints in heaven. In the egalitarian heaven there should be no differences at all. But there can be no doubt that Jesus taught different rewards dependent on how we behaved in this life. We must be careful before we reject the plain teaching of Christ and the apostles in favour of the spirit of the age.

Christ told the story of the steward who was fired and, to make some friends in his new life, immediately started to cancel the debts of those who owed his former master money (Luke 16:1–13). Christ points to the clarity with which the world adjusts its behaviour to inevitable change in order to protect its vital interests. For them it is 'the mammon of unrighteousness', but just as they adjust to worldly reality, we should adjust to the spiritual reality that our reward is in heaven. There would be no point in telling this story if all were to be rewarded in the same way, whether they invested their treasure in the new life or not. The point of the story is that since we know we will not be here for much longer we should build up credit in the life to which we are going.

There is an inclination in rich societies to believe that God rewards us in this life too. They say that if we follow God's ways, we will be rich. They point out that God rewarded the patriarchs, Abraham, Isaac and Jacob, and that he enriched David and Solomon and the other kings who followed him. They point out the greater wealth of the 'Christian countries' and there are many stories of successful Christian businessmen whose hard work and honesty have brought rewards in this life.

But Christ promised no reward on this earth. Instead he promised suffering, that his followers would be cut off from their families and from society, that they would be persecuted and forsaken and might even have to suffer death. The Acts of the Apostles is full of such suffering. Hebrews 11 tells us what happened to the faithful prophets in the hands of their fellow Israelites and the history of martyrdom and suffering in the Christian church down the years fills volumes. The great majority of Christians throughout the years, right down to our own day, have lived in suffering and poverty. They received no reward here, but they will certainly receive it in heaven. The promise of sure riches on this earth is one of the marks of a sect. It should never be the mark of a Christian church.

Of course there are happy times when the church lives in peace and freedom, when the energy and inventiveness which come from the best use of our time and talents bring substantial material reward. But we live in a world full of evil. We must accept that God will judge our society for its evil and so we must sit light to its rewards. It was hard for some of the prophets to accept the message of judgement which they had to pass on to Israel and Judah. After all, it was their own country and they did not want it to be overthrown. Jeremiah said that he did not want to proclaim God's message, but it was like a burning fire and he had to speak. The apostle John was given a vision of a little book, which he was told to eat (Rev 10:9). There is little doubt that the book was God's word. He tells us that it was like honey in his mouth, but it turned his stomach sour. There is a great deal which the church has to say to its own generation that we find good because it is God's word, but which turns our stomachs when we realise the consequences for our own country and our own society.

There is another vision in John's Revelation. It is of the destruction of a great city that clearly symbolises a worldly civilisation. The city's doom causes great distress to 'the kings of the earth who committed adultery with her and shared her luxury' and to 'the merchants of the earth' who 'mourn over her because no one buys their cargo any more'. So do the sea captains and the sailors who earn their living from her, but the angel says, 'By your magic all the nations were led astray. In her was found the blood of the prophets and the saints, and of all who have been killed on the earth' (Rev 18:11–24).

We need to be very clear that, although we are committed to extending God's kingdom on earth and to acting as the salt in society and although we may have positions of responsibility and influence in society, we must never regard it as our final home. Some Christians will be rich for a few years here and some will be poor, some will be honoured in society and others will be killed. Some will be like the patriarchs and David and Solomon, but some will be like Jeremiah, James the brother of John, Peter and Paul and will suffer for Christ's sake.

So, as Christians, we must lay up our treasure in heaven, where moth and rust do not corrupt and where thieves do not break in and steal. If we lay it up in heaven, we will find our reward when we get there. If we try to keep our treasure on earth, we may arrive in heaven, but we will arrive empty-handed and find no reward.

11 What should we give?

The tithe preceded the Mosaic law and survives it

Jesus asked the rich young ruler to sell all he had and give to
the poor, so he went away sad (Mt 19:16–22). But the
apostles did answer the call and give all they had. To some
of us, Christ will give the same unmistakable call, the call
which the rich young man resisted but which the apostles
could not resist. He will call a few of us to sacrifice all our
worldly goods and maybe to a very few, he will call for the
supreme sacrifice of life itself. Those who are specially
called to sacrifice worldly wealth will receive special grace,
will see that they are richer and not poorer. The very few
called to suffer with Christ will feel honoured to be singled
out and Christ himself will take them through the valley of
the shadow of death. But the great majority of us Christians
who are called to live as our neighbours live, will have to
decide exactly how much of our income to give to God's
service and how much to keep for ourselves and our
families.

The first mention of giving part of our wealth to God is
the account of Abraham's gift of a tenth of his booty from
the 'battle of the kings' to Melchizedek:

> Then Melchizedek, King of Salem, brought out bread and
> wine. He was priest of God most high and he blessed
> Abram saying, 'Blessed be Abram by God most high,
> creator of heaven and earth. And blessed be God
> most high, who delivered your enemies into your
> hand.' Then Abram gave him a tenth of everything.
> (Gen 14:18–20)

The second mention is in the story of Abraham's grandson Jacob. After his vision at Bethel, when God promised the land to him and to his descendants, he set up a stone as a pillar and vowed, 'Of all you give me, I will give you a tenth of everything' (Gen 28:22).

Then, five hundred years later, God gave Moses his law. 'A tithe of everything from the land, whether grain from the soil or fruit from the trees, belongs to the Lord; it is holy to the Lord, the entire tithe of the herd and the flock – every tenth animal that passes under the shepherd's rod – will be holy to the Lord' (Lev 27:30–32).

The apostle Paul, writing to the Corinthians does not ask for a fixed amount, but says, 'On the first day of the week, each one of you should set aside a sum of money in keeping with his income, saving it up, so that when I come no collection will have to be made' (1 Cor 16:2).

Our final guideline is in the letter to the Hebrews, where the writer brings us right back to Melchizedek. He quotes Psalm 110, which says of the Messiah, 'You are a priest forever in the order of Melchizedek' and then he says that Jesus has 'become a high priest for ever in the order of Melchizedek.' He goes on (arguing that Christ's priesthood is greater than the priesthood of the Levites),

Now the law requires the descendants of Levi who became priests to collect a tenth from the people – that is their brothers – even though their brothers are descended from Abraham. This man however did not trace his descent from Levi, yet he collected a tenth from Abraham and blessed him who had the promises. (Heb 7:5–6)

What does this passage tell us about tithing? It tells us that since Christ's order of priesthood preceded and succeeded the Mosaic priesthood, the tithe, which illustrates the argument, must also precede and succeed the law. If Abraham gave a tithe to Melchizedek, can we give any less to Christ? We cannot simply dismiss the tithe as a matter purely for the Jewish law. It is, like the ten commandments, something older than the law and something so fundamental that it goes on when the Levitical priesthood has finished.

Paul does not mention a tenth, but surely it cannot be that he expects anyone to give *less*. The only 'scriptures' of the early church were the law and the prophets and Christ's clear command was that the righteousness of his followers had to *exceed* the righteousness of the scribes and Pharisees. Paul does not insist on more, but he can hardly have expected less.

Are there exceptions to the tithe?

Despite these very clear guidelines about giving, we live under the pressures of a materialistic society and we are all very ready to make exceptions for our own particular circumstances. Those with lower than average incomes naturally plead poverty. The young marrieds plead that they need all their income to pay off the mortgage and bring up their children. Pensioners plead that there is nothing left over. But who is poorer than the widow in the temple, whom Jesus commended, saying, 'I tell you the truth, this poor widow has put in more than the others. All the people gave the gifts out of their wealth; but she out of her poverty put in all she had to live on' (Lk 21:3–4)?

Average income in the industrial democracies is ten times the income in the Third World and more than ten times the average income of the early church. If Christians in the early church gave their tenth then and if Third World Christians give their tenth today, surely Christians in Western Europe and North America can give theirs. The industrial democracies are the richest societies in the entire history of the world. Our poorest are richer than the Christians in the early church. How can any of us plead poverty?

Is a tenth so hard? A tenth is the margin of our income.

There is surely no Christian who cannot spend a tenth less than their friends and neighbours outside the church. Are there not *some* things which our neighbours buy that we can do without? We are not asked to cut our spending drastically, just to use a bit less heat, to spend a fraction less on food, have slightly less expensive holidays and fewer drinks, make our clothes and cars last just a bit longer and have homes which are maybe 10% smaller. None of this will kill us, but it might save the life of a child in Africa or the Caribbean.

Tithing gross income

Then, believe it or not, there are those who are in difficulties with the tithe because they are rich! They find themselves in the top tax brackets in a country in which charitable gifts are not tax-deductible. So they argue that progressive taxation aims to produce huge transfers of income from rich to poor, transfers both greater in amount and proportion than at any time in history. That, they say, at least discharges them from the church's duty to look after the needs of the poor. The state looks after that part of the tithe, so they should tithe their net after-tax income, not their gross income.

Though I have met rich people who have put this argument, I have never met one who has troubled to find out how much of the church's income was paid out in relief of poverty before the arrival of the welfare state. I expect that five hundred years ago there were needs for health care, education and welfare which were met by neither state nor church and that, for the most part, those who were sick, illiterate and impoverished simply suffered and often died. I do not see a great burden which used to be borne by the church, of which it is now happily relieved, thereby absolving us of part of our duty to pay a tenth of our income before making any deductions. The Jews of Christ's time were obliged to pay both their tithe and the Roman tax. Jesus chided them for not paying the full tithe and he himself paid the Roman tax (Mt 17:24–27).

Of course a combination of inflation and progressive taxation with unchanged tax thresholds can be very painful. In the mid 1970s British executives found themselves with 25% inflation, a wage freeze and a top tax rate of 83% on earned income (it was 98% on investment income). Only 30% of the tithe was tax-deductible – and then only if legally covenanted for seven years. If Christians can tithe through that, they can tithe through anything.

In fact most rich countries today allow tax deductions for giving to registered charities. In North America the regimes are liberal. In Britain the covenant has to be for four years and, after a period in which the full deduction of tax was allowed to be offset against taxed income, the deduction is now only allowed for the basic rate of tax. Those tithing incomes taxed at higher rates are once more squeezed, but the top rate is now 60% instead of 83%.

In most of the industrial democracies, giving can be made through charitable trusts without any difficulty. Even in Britain, where it has to be covenanted for four years, there are escape clauses if we lose our jobs or our income drops drastically and the Charities Aid Foundation is full of good advice to those who need to tailor their covenant to their own particular needs.

I believe that each of us should do our best to take advantage of tax allowances to increase our giving. It is absurd for anyone who pays the standard rate of tax to put more than token cash in the church collection each Sunday, when allowable tax deduction can add 20% or 30% to the amount given. Churches which find themselves with more cash income than tax deductible income should not only tell their members, but make it as easy as possible for them to claim tax deduction and give them a special cheque to put in the Sunday collections.

Set aside regularly and keep it separate and sacred

Paul told the Corinthians to set aside their money as they earned it, so that there would be no collections when he came (1 Cor 16:2). This is still a wise and necessary discipline. Moses told Israel that the tithe was holy. It was God's and not to be touched. So, as soon as we get our income, we should put our tithe where it cannot be touched again. If it all goes to the church, it should be paid over as soon as we receive it. If it goes to a trust under covenant, we should give our bank standing instructions to pay it the day after our monthly income cheque is due.

We should never mix the tithe with ordinary income and try to accumulate it in our ordinary bank account. If we do, we will almost certainly find, when we come to pay it over, that we have spent it on something else. But if we pay it to a trust or, at least, to a separate tithe account in the bank, we will always find that we have plenty to give when we are asked for a donation. It is far easier to respond generously with a cheque from a full tithe account than it is to write out a cheque from our hard-pressed ordinary account. I am a trained accountant, yet I have never, since we married and started tithing, dared to mix the tithe with our ordinary bank account.

Paul did not want to arrive in Corinth and find the money already spent and neither did he want fundraising to dominate his visit. There would be other important issues he wanted to discuss. There is all the difference in the world between explaining the need to a church whose members have already accumulated the money and trying to persuade a church to give when the money is still in their pockets. The visitor's proper job should be to explain the need and the church's to decide how to allocate their money between that need and others. But a visitor to a church which has set nothing aside must undertake the additional pastoral work of persuading the church to be generous. He is made to plead for money and is tempted to use emotional pressure to push his cause hard, knowing that, since the money still has to be raised, his success may damage other causes with less eloquent advocates.

It may please the church to make their visitors beg, but it is not a healthy relationship. A church should have a secure income, should be able to look after all the causes which have come to depend on it and should have enough over for special causes without damaging those which it supports regularly.

Regular giving leads to regular money management. Most of us, rich and poor, tend to waste money; but tithing makes us more careful, so we can probably pay our tithe out of the money we no longer waste. The need to find the 10% means that we look at the other 90% more carefully. We look first of all at what we can save, but we may go on to look at how much more we could earn. It can be one of the factors which pushes Christians out of a low-paid but undemanding job into one which is tougher but more productive. A great many of those who have begun to tithe agree with the saying that 'The 90% always seems to go further than the 100% did before.' It is not just that the Lord honours those who honour him, but that he also makes us look at the expenditure we are wasting and at the income we could earn if we exerted ourselves.

Money management

Anyone who has kept a shop knows that those who have least money are not always the most careful about how they spend it. And the very rich, who seem to have least need to be careful, are often the ones who count their money most carefully and only part with it if they can find a real bargain. A friend of ours was taken out to lunch by a rich Swiss banker. When the bill came, the banker checked all the items against the menu and then carefully checked the addition and the percentage for tax and service at the end.

Christians should be neither among the improvident poor nor the extravagant rich. If we put a stopwatch on our time to find out where we waste it, we should keep accounts to find out where we waste our money. Most of us could cut our phone bill by 10%. We might need to buy a timer, but it would quickly pay for itself. It shouldn't be hard to make a car last longer or to drive it for a 10% saving in fuel. We could care for our clothes so that they lasted a few months longer. A money-saving diet would make most of us healthier and 10% less on heating our homes would keep us more vigorous.

Saving money in the Third World usually needs collective action by the church. An old friend of ours gave us a graphic picture of his country under a corrupt military dictatorship. There was a three-figure rate of inflation and the salaries in the state medical service where he worked were fixed as were the official prices of most staple commodities. As a result everything was traded on the black market. Few of the drugs ever got through to the hospitals and patients had to buy them on the black market if they wanted treatment. The doctors could not keep their wives and families and most of them demanded fees from their patients in the 'free' health service, but our friend did not feel he could honourably do this.

Things came to a head in a strike of the national health service. The dictator sent in troops and terrorised the hospitals. My friend went with his colleagues to protest to him and told him that, as a professed Christian, he should see the harm he was doing and resign. The dictator frankly explained that he could not resign because he was not sure that a successor government would grant immunity for what he had done. Next day our friend applied to go on a medical course abroad and was granted a visa at once. Later there was a *coup d'état*, the dictator was shot, but the succeeding regime was no better.

Talking over this case with our friend afterwards, it was clear that he and others like him in ex-colonial territories still pinned their hopes on finding a political solution. But Christians in communist countries have little hope of that. They do not have rampant inflation, but they have the same

shortages and black markets because of the incredibly
bureaucratic central planning. Another friend of ours was a
production manager in a tractor plant. He asked whether it
was right for a Christian to sign an urgent request for a
hundred times as many spare parts as he needed, since it
was the only way to keep the plant going. I think I told him
that that was the responsibility of his boss, but it did not
really deal with what would happen if he were the boss.
Next time I saw him I asked what had happened. He said
that they had set up their own system within the district.
The farmers wanted tractors, the tractor plant wanted spare
parts and the spare parts plant workers wanted food.
So they had a triangular exchange outside the monetary
system.

It seems to me that in countries where the system is
corrupt or impossibly rigid, the members of the church
may need to act collectively. Where incomes are low,
productivity is also low and collective action by church
members can have a most dramatic effect. There have been
some most successful church-inspired projects which have
turned poverty-stricken communities into successful farming ones. The need to keep to God's law and not to conform
to the world has been the dynamic which has urged
Christians on to change the conditions in which they find
themselves. On the other hand there are rising middle-class
communities which have still not learnt the financial
discipline of regular giving, let alone regular tithing. They
conform to the conditions they find around them and do
not see the need to find ways of setting Christian standards
wherever Christians meet together as a church.

Supergiving for super incomes

Rich Christians should not only give a tenth of their income, they should consider whether to give more. Robert
Laidlaw, a New Zealand businessman, decided that if his
business succeeded, he should give an increased share of

his income to God's work. He drew up a progressive scale, starting with 10%. As his income rose to the next level, so the percentage would rise, first to 20%, then to 30%, 40% and 50%. He told us that as soon as he had done this, his income started rising rapidly towards the top percentage. He felt that God was saying to him that, since he had been taken into partnership, he was blessing the business. Though that may sound a rather familiar way of putting it, Jesus told us that whoever honours him, he will honour. Who is God more likely to trust with worldly wealth, those who spend it on themselves or those who return a tenth or more to the God who gave it them?

John Laing, who built a small family business into one of Britain's four largest construction companies, was a very simple man. He believed that his great prosperity had come because God knew that he would look after the wealth he had been given. He gave the greater part to Christian work and did not try to impose his own views on how the money should be spent. He felt that that was for those who were more qualified than he was. Other rich Christians tell the same story. They recognise that they may not have many sparkling gifts – though some, like Robert Laidlaw, would shine in any company – but their God relies on them to be careful with his money. They do not waste it on high personal spending, nor do they allow their own whims or prestige to govern the use of their donations, but they act on the best advice they can find.

We cannot outgive God

Above all, these are men and women of faith. They believe that God is the giver of all and that he has the power to care for those who care for him. A gift to God's service is a safer reserve than cash in the bank, for God knows our future needs better than we do and, while cash can be eaten up by inflation or even disappear in a bank failure, God's resources are not limited. Just as God answers prayer and looks after the needs of pioneer missionaries, so he looks after the needs of those who give. As the psalmist says, 'I have been young and now am old, yet I have never seen the righteous forsaken or their children begging bread' (Ps 37:25).

The prophet Malachi told the Jews just returned from exile that they were robbing God and that they should 'bring the tithes into the storehouse' (Mal 3:10). No doubt they all felt the need to rebuild the prosperity of Jerusalem, not to mention their own prosperity, as fast as they could. Nehemiah, the governor, had to prevent them from trading all through the sabbath day by closing the city gates. They doubtless said that every penny was needed. But Malachi told them that God knew their needs. The Lord Almighty was telling them:

> Test me in this and see if I will not throw open the floodgates of heaven and pour out so much blessing that you will not have room enough for it. I will prevent pests from devouring your crops and the vines in the fields will not cast your fruit. Then all the nations will call you blessed for yours will be a delightful land (Mal 3:10–12).

There is one sure way of finding out whether these promises of God are true and that is to put them to the test. Those who have paid 'the whole tithe' say that they are true. But there is nothing like trying it out for ourselves. If we give 5% now, then all the full tenth needs is another 5% of our incomes. That's not a very expensive investment, so why don't we try it and see?

Tithing gifts and legacies

I know the depths of resistance to tithing. In my year as president of Britain's Fellowship of Independent Evangelical Churches, I gave addresses in about fifteen regions up and down the country. Since I was a deacon, which was unusual for a president, I thought I would speak on tithing at the evening address. Ministers tend to avoid the subject. They probably feel that they will be thought to have a vested interest in a higher church income.

In the morning I spoke on the ten commandments and, as I shook hands at the door, each person would say something polite: 'Very interesting', or 'Most helpful'. But after the evening address on tithing, they couldn't get out of the door fast enough. If I caught anyone's eye, I got a shifty look and a curt 'Goodnight'. But a few wrote afterwards to say that they were starting to tithe. I also heard that a number of churches which had paid their ministers a most disgracefully low salary had reformed and that others, who had had no minister had now decided that they could afford to call one.

There are those who accept the principle of the tithe, but who, whether consciously or not, regard certain forms of income as 'tithe exempt'. They might not put it quite like that, but it is perhaps because they do not look at their income with the same beady eye as the tax collector, who overlooks nothing.

Do we, for instance, tithe the gifts and legacies which we receive? And if not, why not? Often we were not even expecting them and it shouldn't be too difficult to do with 90% of what we were not expecting, instead of 100%.

Then there are those who either forget about capital gains or regard these too as 'tithe deductible', maybe on the grounds that they are no more than a compensation for inflation. However we should note that the first recorded tithe, given by Abram to Melchizedek, was a capital gain and though Abram might not have faced inflation in the pastoral economy of those days, he could, no doubt, have argued for a reserve against potential losses to marauding neighbours.

Christ chided the Pharisees for tithing the produce of their herb gardens and 'neglecting the weightier matters of the law'. So we do not want to be pedantic about small things while neglecting the greater. We are trustees of our

income and capital for Christ and when we look at it to see
what is due each year, we should look with the careful eyes
of trustees, making absolutely sure that we are caring for
the true interests of the real owner, who has given us his
trust.

Christ set higher standards than the law

It is easy enough to be a hypocrite until the collection plate
comes round. That is what sorts out the adults in the faith
from the children, the true faith from the bogus, and the
real believer from the hypocrite. Only those who are
serious in their faith will put real money into it. For the rest,
their faith is only worth their loose change. They fight
against the 'legalism' of the tithe because an exact figure
punctures their self-image of open-handed generosity.
Giving makes us feel good, it puts us ahead of those who do
not give, it adds to our stock of virtue and we do not like
people who deflate us by saying that our manifest goodness
is not good enough. 'Of course', we tell ourselves, 'we are
not plaster saints, but we do our best.' We hope that in the
final judgement God will draw up a divine balance sheet
and decide that with all our commitments and in all the
circumstances, we really have done our best. The last thing
we want is some busybody bustling in now and setting a
10% pass mark before our time is up!

Christ set higher standards than the law. He has given us
a new law, the law of love. The scribes and Pharisees turned
the law into a lowest common denominator which even the
rich young ruler felt he had kept from his youth up. Christ
has turned it into a highest common factor of love – a level at
which all of us realise that we fail, but to which the Holy
Spirit compels the Christian and for which he gives us
supernatural strength.

12   Where should we give?

Our church has first call on our tithe

There are Christians who see no need to belong to any particular church. They float between one and the other, reflecting the rootlessness and lack of commitment of worldly society. Even if they attend one church fairly regularly, they do not want to feel tied down to it. Otherwise a deacon might actually ask them to do something for the church. And many rich Christians do not want to commit all their giving to the church they attend on Sunday. They prefer to look after their own financial affairs.

But the church is the institution ordained by God for Christians. The writer to the Hebrews tells us not to neglect our gathering together with fellow Christians (Heb 10:25). We should all be under the spiritual authority of the elders of the church, who are to look after our spiritual welfare. In our secular individualistic society, the three institutions given by God for the ordering of human society, the state, the church and the family, are all under attack. Nothing ultimately matters except the freedom of the individual and no institution should stand in our way. So it is not surprising that even Christians are carried along by this mood. But from the beginning to the end of the New Testament, the church is central to Christian activity. Paul collected money from one church, the church in Corinth, to give to another church, the church in Jerusalem.

The Christian church is our collective witness to the world. Scattered individuals have some influence in human society, but the real and lasting impact is made by collective activity. In politics we are organised into political parties, in wage-bargaining we organise into trade unions – whether some people like it or not – in economic activity we organise into companies. The political party, the trade union and the corporation are all much more effective than any individual could ever be. All of those bodies are useful, but the church is not only useful, it is divinely ordained. We can refuse to join a political party or a trade union and we can insist on working on our own, but if we are Christians, we must be members of a church, which has elders and deacons, where the Word of God is taught and the sacraments are administered.

And if we are members of the church, we must support it. If we are seen to spend our money on our own houses to the neglect of the church, our priorities are noted. David wanted to build the temple because he thought it wrong that he should have a roof over his head while the ark of God was in a tent (2 Sam 7:2). Although God does not live in the church, it is a building sacred to him and we should look after it. It is a disgrace to our Christian witness to keep our church building shabby and badly repaired, the inside cold and draughty and the seats uncomfortable, while all the Christians live in well-kept, warm and comfortable houses. It is an even greater disgrace when the church has to raise money for repairs from those who are not Christians.

There is, perhaps one exception. I believe that Christians are entitled to raise outside money for historic church buildings, whose cost of repair and upkeep is totally out of proportion to their service to the local Christian community. From the top of our house we can see, fifteen miles away across the flat fenland, the two towers of the great old cathedral of Ely. The Christians in that small market town cannot possibly be expected to keep that great medieval monument in repair and they are, quite rightly, asking the community for the money.

Fair pay for church workers

A church is also judged by its treatment of those who work for it. The world puts its money where its heart is and will pay for whatever it thinks important. So the world will not take our commitment to our faith seriously if we do not pay our clergy and other church workers well.

How often we hear people say, 'But it is the Lord's money and we must be careful.' What they really mean is that if the church is not careful about its commitments, the members will have to find more of their own money. I have spent long years sitting on committees arguing with enthusiasts who want to take on this or that exciting project, that our own workers are our first commitment and that we must not take on anything new at their expense.

It is odd how easily those who have to pay can turn the moral argument on its head and argue as if *they* were the ones receiving the money. They say, 'We as Christians should not go into full-time Christian service to make money.' But it is not they who are in full-time service. They are the ones who are making money and it is their responsibility to see that the dedication of those going into full-time service is not exploited.

The whole teaching of the Bible is in favour of generosity and against meanness. It is said time and again in the Proverbs. Our Lord says it and Paul says it. Those who engage other people for Christian work should be generous. So it is *not* spiritual to be mean. We should leave it to those to whom generous salaries are offered to decide whether it is spiritual to receive them. They may well ask for less. My father-in-law, who was the minister of a large London church, felt that it would be wrong for him to receive more than ministers in small churches. But they should make the decision and not have it imposed upon them.

We not only need to see that salaries are appropriate, we should also look after housing, cars, sick care and pensions in the same spirit; and if the church owns the rectory or manse, there should be enough left over to provide for a retirement home. And if the church does own the home of the minister and his wife, they should not fuss about the repairs. Much better to give the minister a generous allowance for repairs and let him and his wife decide themselves what needs to be done. The care of the church, studying, preaching, advising, guiding, comforting, rebuking, reconciling and patient listening are quite enough to do without worrying about what happens in old age and to dependants left behind after death.

Of course there *are* those who are guilty of the sin of simony and who make money out of human superstition, gullibility and guilt. Not only are there notorious sects which are set up to do this and whose leaders are very rich, but there are nominally Christian churches which step over the line that divides a church from a sect. If a church leader becomes very rich and his lifestyle and church building programme are out of all proportion to those of other ministers and other churches, then we have to question whether he leads a church or a cult. If we see a TV service where more time is given to fundraising and personality promotion than to the gospel, then something is badly wrong.

'Double honour'

The Christian life should be one of balance. Paul, writing to Timothy about the payment of the elders, says, 'The elders who direct the affairs of the church well are worthy of double honour, especially those whose work is preaching and teaching' (1 Tim 5:17).

What kind of honour is it which Paul wants the church to double? Well he is clearly talking about money, since he goes on to argue in terms of reward and wages, 'For the Scripture says, "Do not muzzle the ox while it is treading out the grain," and "The worker deserves his wages"' (1 Tim 5:18).

If 'honour' is financial reward, then 'double honour' must mean double the normal financial reward. A commonsense practical interpretation would give the teaching elder double the average salary of the congregation.

There are some who cannot conceive of any full-time church worker earning more than they do. But why not? The world honours its leaders with higher pay, why should the church not do the same? Even if not all church leaders have a university degree, they will have spent some years in study. They should, at least, rank with the other professionals in society. Impoverished clergy are a disgrace to the church. To honour God's servant is to honour God.

But a differential of two times average earnings also avoids undue affluence and ostentation. In the Third World today there should not be too much difference between pastors, whether local or expatriate, and the churches they serve. The pioneer missionary, Hudson Taylor, persuaded his colleagues to wear Chinese dress and live in Chinese style. There is no need for an expatriate to keep to first world standards of expenditure in a Third World country. First world standards of health and hygiene help the job and avoid crippling illness, but an air-conditioned missionary compound separates the expatriates from the church and people they are meant to serve.

A tithing church should have no difficulty in affording a minister or in giving 'double honour'. Twenty wage-earners should be able to pay the same salary as they earn themselves and also look after heating and maintenance; forty should be able to give 'double honour'. Churches need an elder who can, as Paul says, 'live of the gospel' (1 Cor 9:14). The teaching elder needs time to study, time to talk to other ministers. The person engaged in pastoral ministry needs time to listen patiently to the troubles and problems of the church member and to all those who come to the church for help. Even with the part-time help that is available for sick visiting, youth groups and house groups, there needs to be someone who has the care of the church as first priority and

who has the time to accept the commitments which that
priority brings.

'Widows and orphans'

The world may see the church simply as the building where
people spend an hour together on Sunday and where
nothing much happens for the rest of the week. But Christ
told the apostles that the sign by which all men should be
able to distinguish his followers was that 'you love one
another' (Jn 13:34). The letters of the apostles spell out the
consequences of that love.

The church was to care for the widows and the children
who had no family to look after them. If there were
nephews or grown children who could earn, then they
should not be a charge on the church. If there were younger
widows, they could marry again, but the older widows
should be taken care of by the church and should, so far as
they were able, help in the work of the church.

Although the industrial democracies have a great deal of
state welfare, many countries still have huge gaps in the
welfare system. But the main gap is not in state funding, it
is the loss of active family support for those in need. Under
pressure from the beliefs of humanism, aided by the greed
of hedonistic materialism, the family is splitting apart. It is
not just that the divorce rate has soared, but the number of
unmarried mothers and one-parent families has soared.
Even the grandparents, to whom the daughter used to take
her small children when her husband walked out, are themselves divorced. And when grandparents are too feeble to
look after themselves, they are dumped in an old folk's
home and those of them who have visitors are the lucky
ones. So, despite the welfare state, the church has the job of
looking after those of its members who are part of the
driftwood from our shipwrecked society.

In societies which, though socially richer, are materially
poorer, the church still has a major role, in the New

Testament style, in looking after the widows and orphans who do not have families to help them and the church also helps the sick and helpless who cannot help themselves. However poor the church may be, it is richer than those who have nothing.

Help to poor churches

The apostle Paul also teaches that rich churches have a duty towards poor churches. He raised money from the churches in Greece to help the poor churches in Jerusalem. The great eighteenth-century evangelist, George Whitefield, travelled repeatedly across the Atlantic to raise money from the rich churches in England to help the poor churches in America found an orphanage in Georgia. As we read of the tremendous impact of Whitefield's preaching, we wonder at the seemingly marginal cause of all that travelling. But it was not marginal to George Whitefield.

We must not give patronisingly to poorer churches. We may be rich only because the gospel came to our country, leading our ancestors to a disciplined and committed life which has made our generation rich. But our rich societies are now busy breaking up all that they ever stood for and we have unleashed the bloodiest wars the world has ever known, so we are not universally admired. Therefore we have no right to insist that our way of spending the money is the only way.

On the other hand poverty does not ban the sin of covetousness. Money talks – and the difference between serving God in your own poor country and going to America on a scholarship can be just too tempting. The brain drain from the Third World to the rich democracies is not confined to secular jobs. Many good Christians never go back and the problem of re-entry is often worse than the culture-shock of the newly arrived expatriate missionary, for whom the local church is always prepared to make allowances.

Culture talks too. Some Christians can be deeply influenced by the lethargy and fatalism of the cultures in which they live. There are churches which make commitments that are not fulfilled, whose middle class do not accept responsibility for fundraising, where staff are taken on and salaries are left unpaid, who argue that after all, the rich countries have more money, so their churches should provide. Sin and temptation know no frontiers.

We should perhaps be especially careful with appeals to raise money for persecuted Christians in communist countries. As an elder in an East European church once said to me, 'What do they do with the money they raise, because money cannot solve the problem?' A pastor from another East European country said, 'Our authorities know about the Bible smuggling, but they let it go on, both because it saves hard currency and also because it gives them a case against the churches which take the Bibles should they ever want to use it.' All of the East Europeans we know make the point that no one in a Warsaw Pact country wants to be found in the pay of a NATO country. It is hard enough for a church to persuade the authorities that it is not using its unique country-wide organisation and its weekly sermons to undermine the government, but to be found taking money covertly from the NATO powers would kill completely their case that the good Christian is a particularly good citizen.

The churches in communist countries do need help, but they want it to be overt, legal and according to the guidelines which govern their relations with the state. A good many ministers from Western Europe are now allowed to make visits to churches in Eastern Europe and even East Germany has begun to allow western visitors. So we should help them, but it is best to do it through recognised church channels and not through today's Scarlet Pimpernels!

None of these cautions are arguments against sending money from rich churches to poor ones. They are cautions against believing that money is the answer to every problem, and they are arguments for looking at the causes of

poverty and deciding what is the best way to help. The old
Chinese proverb said, 'If you give a hungry man a fish, he
will be hungry again tomorrow, but if you teach him how to
fish, he will never be hungry again.' Paul's fundraising was
for famine relief. The Christians in Judea could not help
themselves because the crops had failed. Money had to be
given to keep them alive and to enable them to sow again.
What had happened in Judea could happen next year in
Achea or in Macedonia. In that case the churches in Judea
would be expected to come, in turn, to the help of their
brothers in Greece.

Famine and disaster relief and medical aid

The case for famine and disaster relief is as strong as it was
in Paul's day. If money is not raised today, people will be
dead tomorrow. When the Ethiopian crops failed in 1984,
grain ships in the Indian ocean were diverted at once to its
ports. Earthquakes and eruptions bring air-lifted supplies
at once. And there is a strong case for sending money
through the network of the churches, who will handle
it honestly and will make sure that help gets through to
those who really need it. If the churches cannot handle it
themselves, they can send aid through trusted non-
governmental agencies. These agencies, known for short as
NGOs, are playing an increasing part in distributing aid to
the Third World. Donor governments find that their
government to government aid is too often siphoned off
and ends up for sale on the market-place for those who
have money enough to buy. So they give through NGOs
who can make conditions or even refuse aid without
creating a diplomatic incident.

Christ not only fed the poor, he also healed the sick and
there is a great deal that rich churches can do to help poor
churches look after the sick in their communities and also to
keep them healthy. Medical missions were a beginning.
Most are now served by nationals, but expatriates can still

help with training in clinics and hospitals and rich churches
can help with supplies of medical equipment and drugs, of
which Third World hospitals are chronically short.

Mission

The last instruction of Christ to the leaders he was to leave
behind was that they should 'go and make disciples of all
nations, baptising them in the name of the Father and of the
Son and of the Holy Spirit, and teaching them to obey
everything I have commanded you. And surely I am with
you always, to the very end of the age' (Mt 28:19,20).

This final 'great commission' of Jesus must be one of the
primary obligations of the Christian church and so it must
be one of the primary charges on the giving of each church.

As with the early church, so today, a great deal of the
missionary activity of the church takes place at home. Most
people become Christians through friends and a great deal
of the conversation is casual and takes place in each other's
houses. Even the slightly more formal 'house group' does
not need money. But churches should reach out beyond the
social circle of their members. Suburban churches should
remember the inner cities, towns should remember the
villages and, as they begin to make effort, they will begin to
need part-time and then full-time workers and finally they
will need buildings.

This local outreach is hard work and some churches work
for a long time before seeing any results. It is tempting for
churches to put their money and effort into the more
spectacular 'evangelist mission' with big names and a huge
supporting cast. But the big mission can only reap what has
already been sown. If nothing has been sown, there will be
nothing to reap. And big missions need big money, which
is all too often taken away from the less spectacular efforts.

One regular pattern to church outreach starts with a
Sunday school which is set up in temporary buildings on a
new housing development. The parents come to special

occasions and get to know the teachers. Then services are held, maybe once a month, for parents and children together. Some parents become Christians and the church sends some of its own members to join them to form a new church. The church is joined by Christians moving into the new development and the members make their own network of friends, some of whom become Christians. Then they decide to build their own building and a new church is founded with the help of the old. I have opened several churches set up in that pattern and it is a real privilege. The local mayor came to one opening service and told me, 'I don't go much to church, but I know all that this new church has done for my people here, so what they have to say must be worth listening to.'

Overseas mission has been a prime object of church giving for the last hundred and fifty years. In that time the gospel has circled the earth and there are now Christian churches in almost every country in the world. Just as the first churches were formed by missionaries who were able to travel freely within the great Roman Empire, so the missions of the last century and a half have for better or worse, followed imperial power. But in the last forty years all those empires have been dissolved and expatriate missionaries, especially those from former imperial powers, are not now so welcome. In some Muslim countries and in most communist countries they are not welcome at all and even where they are, the work they can do is strictly limited.

Yet the need is as great as ever. There are huge and growing populations who have never heard the Christian gospel. There are many countries where the old type of expatriate missionary is still welcome, but there are also quite new ways of helping to spread the Christian message and help the new churches.

One of the best ways of spreading the Christian gospel in the world as it is today is through student evangelism. It is the mission to which I and my wife have committed our own time and energy. Immediately after the second world war, the International Fellowship of Evangelical Students was born, bringing together the few countries which had an organised evangelical student movement. They included Norway, the United Kingdom, Canada, Australia, the United States, Switzerland, the Netherlands and the Republic of China.

China was lost to the IFES within three years, but everywhere else student mission has grown fast and now there are seventy-seven affiliated national movements, with pioneer work in other countries which do not yet have a self-supporting national movement.

No government has yet been able to find a way of preventing students from exchanging ideas with each other – other than by closing the universities. So no authority can prevent Christian students from telling their friends about the Christian gospel. They have access which no local church can have, let alone a foreign mission. The university is a place in which new ideas are learnt and students' minds are open and interested. And the students are the future leaders of their country, the future teachers, journalists, church leaders, civil servants and politicians. There is no more cost-effective mission than student mission.

Nor can IFES, governed by its general committee from seventy-seven national movements, ever be accused of representing one part of the world or one political ideology. And the field staff who pioneer and help to set up new movements come from all over the world. A Brazilian staff worker has gone to help the Christian students in Angola. A Chinese staff worker helps the new movements in South-East Asia. A Dutch staff worker pioneered the new movement in Austria and an American staff worker the new movement in Spain.

The twelve student and graduate summer schools, in which my wife and I have helped, bring back a kaleidoscope of memories – Latin Americans, who really know how to play guitars, arguing fiercely about liberation theology; two very tall and dignified Africans from the Dinko tribe in Southern Sudan, four South Africans, one from each race, who all came together; a Japanese girl with a glorious mezzo-soprano voice, who bowed respectfully to everyone and who had been brought up in one of the main Shinto shrines in Kyoto, where her father was the chief priest; an Arab-Israeli girl, who, after listening to discussions on the Christian teaching on relations between men and women, decided that she was going to have a say in choosing her husband; a Danish girl from the Faroe Islands arguing passionately about women's rights; a group of new Christians from Austria who wanted to get to the bottom of every Christian doctrine and would not be put off by shallow answers; an Austrian boy and a Polish girl, each with their arm round the other, the spare hand holding a German/Polish dictionary (they eventually married); a big American group, who did a song and dance act with impeccable choreography; a Scot who brought the house down with his kilt, sporran and bonnet; an Egyptian girl whose profile looked as if it had come straight off a temple frieze in Luxor. Suddenly, as we sing and pray together, the universal church of Christ becomes a living reality.

We all learn from each other. And we learn what we could not possibly learn from Christians of our own nation and culture. What we find startling as we begin discussing Christian issues, is how impregnated we all are with the culture of our own society. The Scandinavians and the Californians are gently but firmly told that they are putting the views of their society on the position of women and not Christian views. The Africans find that they cannot defend traditional African views of the position of women either. The Latin American advocates of liberation theology are asked whether they believe that the Czech students should start throwing stones at Soviet tanks. And so we force each other to throw off the cultural bias and look without prejudice at the actual Christian teaching and we all go home with a far clearer vision of our mutual faith.

Student work is important, but it cannot cover the ground. We still need foreign missions and they need some expatriate missionaries. It may be that some have to go as doctors and teachers, as experts on pest control or as irrigation engineers; but there are huge populations, especially in Asia, who have never heard the Christian gospel, and we still need to take it to them.

The style of missions is changing. They work much more closely with and within the local churches. They have seen how much the church in China has grown in the last forty years and they know that continued dependence on the missionary does not make for a strong church. Those who give to missions should not insist that every year should show results. There is a time for breaking ground, a time for sowing with no evident results and then, perhaps years later, a time of great reaping. The work needs perseverance as new missionaries slowly learn the strange language and culture, as the Bible is translated into tribal dialects and as fierce opposition is endured and overcome. So the churches which fund the missions should not expect quick results, but should keep closely in touch, praying, writing and encouraging.

The cure of social ills

Some churches, especially those in the centre of big cities, are surrounded by the problems of alcoholism, drug abuse, violence and threatened suicide. These problems and the problems of the break-up of the family are everywhere overwhelming the social workers, who cannot, in any case, give the moral answers which go to the root of the problems. No church can ignore these human agonies on its very doorstep. A church which is not seen to care about the pressing needs of society will not be asked by society about its hidden but even greater spiritual needs.

Jesus did not separate his love for men's eternal welfare from his love for their daily needs. His love compelled him to meet every need. When his disciples told him to send the crowds away after the sermon, he said that they had had nothing to eat and would faint on the way without it, so they had to be fed first (Mt 14:15–21). He healed because his love compelled him to heal and to free those whom 'Satan has bound' (Lk 13:16). He was the creator who had 'made all things good' and felt compelled to use his power to restore what had been spoilt.

We find that the emphasis of the apostles in the letters to the early churches is on doctrine and its implications for Christian behaviour. They are told to show love in all that they do and it must have been the contrast between this unselfish love and a selfish society which brought their neighbours in such numbers to the early churches and to faith in Christ.

God who made the soul made the body too, and he has promised to redeem both soul and body. Christ has told us that, after the first command to love God, is the second: to love our neighbour as ourselves. When asked by a cynic, 'Who is my neighbour?' he told the story of the good Samaritan (Lk 10:25–37). The Samaritans were not of the same race or religion as the Jews, but the story tells of a Samaritan who cared for the wounded Jew as a neighbour – and the unspoken moral was that the Jews were to do the same for them. We all have neighbours today who are in desperate need of help.

Divorce now ends one marriage in three, and already in some places the number is approaching one in two. There is also a sharp rise in the number of children born to un-married parents. So there is a rapidly increasing number of one-parent families. As one bereft woman said, 'This is worse than being a widow.' The widow or widower has memories of a faithful partner, but the deserted partner has nothing but a slap in the face, a hard blow to their self-esteem and self-confidence. And the children are brought up feeling that one parent didn't care about them.

The children react. More spectacular than the loneliness of the deserted parent is the soaring juvenile crime rate, linked by social studies to the soaring number of broken partnerships. As a leading policeman said, 'If there are not a father and mother to keep two children in order, how can one of my men keep two thousand in order?' The streets are no longer safe. Old women are attacked, robbed and sometimes killed for pocket money. There is the new crime of wanton destruction, known as vandalism. And it is getting worse every year as society slowly destabilises.

The church can help. A friend of ours started a club for teenage gangs. She didn't mean to. She had bought an old chapel in a poor area of London to store copies of a Christian magazine, of which she was editor, and the local children arrived at the door. They said it was a chapel and used to have a Sunday school. So she started one for them. Then the first teenage gang arrived and she started a youth club and asked for members of our church to help. Next came the first gang's local rivals. She stood by the door and each gave up his knives to her as he came in. She kept them all by arranging separate evenings for each gang. They all came from broken homes and their only loyalty was to the gang, but they needed something more and she gave it to them. She taught them the Christian faith and they listened because they respected her. When the police made an indiscriminate raid and took them in for something they had not done, they sent for her and the police learnt to respect her too. But when they were wrong, she told them. When they were older, she found them jobs and did her best to see that they kept them.

Not only the young arrive at the open church door. In downtown churches, the drunks will certainly come. Churches are warm, there is often hot coffee after services and there are places to sit out of the wind. They bring their troubles with them. When they feel disgusted with themselves, they can convince everyone, including themselves, that they really want to start again. But even if they stay sober, they have huge problems to face in finding and then holding a job. Usually they cannot stand the pressure and the whole cycle starts all over again. Drugs are an even greater problem. In both cases the church needs skilled and medically experienced help and a separate and safe area in

the church buildings. But the church can give what the
social worker cannot, the gospel. The experience of
churches with both drink and drugs is that a true Christian
faith can give the will to cure addiction. That is not the
object of faith, it is a by-product. Nor is the will, even of a
Christian, rock-steady. But Christ cares for both soul and
body and it is, as Christ himself taught, those who have
come to an end of their own resources who are most likely
to find faith.

The mentally subnormal also head for the church's open
door. If one in twenty of the church's congregation has not
had a mental problem, then the church does not reflect a
proper cross-section of society. In fact a church should have
more than its fair share, because it is likely to give a
welcome which those with confused minds are unlikely to
find anywhere else. We are to love all our neighbours,
whatever their condition, and where no one else wants to
know them we have a special obligation. They come in all
kinds of conditions, and someone needs to know enough
about the condition of each to be able to establish relations.
The need of the church to care for the mentally subnormal
has increased since health authorities have decided that it is
better for most of them to be in society rather than in mental
institutions. The problem is that society does not make
them welcome and so more of them are turning to the
churches for help.

Promotion of Christian standards in society

The relation between church and state has never been easy
and it has certainly never been stable, but there is little
doubt that government does need some agreed moral order
in society, some standard of conduct for all those relations
between people which cannot be regulated by the law
courts and some ultimate moral authority which will guide
the law-makers themselves. For over a thousand years,
since the dark ages gave way to the middle ages, Christianity has been that ultimate authority, first in Europe and

then also in America. There has been a repeated cycle of religious revival which sharpened public perception of Christian standards, followed by corruption as public understanding dulled again. But each peak has seemed to be higher than the last, so that there has been a steady increase in human dignity and in the moral order.

But at present we are in a deep trough. In an age of moral relativism, it has been harder and harder to win the argument for Christian standards. But a great many people are beginning to wake up to the horror of our disintegrating society. It is clear that science can no longer be the ultimate moral arbiter, but that scientists themselves need the strongest possible moral guidelines. They invented the nuclear weapon, but could not put limits on its use. And as they begin to look at the use of human embryos, it is clear that some moral guidance higher than the physical sciences is needed.

Nor are the social sciences any more reassuring. They seem capable of taking away the old disciplines, which kept society together, without putting any compelling moral order in their place. The intellectuals do not carry the same moral sanctions as the church did. They can say what people ought to do in their long-term self-interest, but they find it hard to counter the natural tendency to live for today. They will not admit that there is a corrosive principle of evil at large, which needs something much tougher than textbooks on social science to stop it.

So the family, which is the oldest and most basic social institution of society, is now dissolving. Materialism is increasing, making it hard for society's leaders to use the enormous potential of science and engineering to create jobs and wealth. All the old optimism has gone and nostalgia is big business. Alcohol and drugs are used to escape from the problems and every kind of superstition is back in business. And over all is the threat of the bomb and the final destruction of our civilisation.

It is small wonder that Christians are working hard to put the Christian guidelines back again. But we have a great deal of work to do. We have to win the intellectual argument, because that is the argument we have lost. We have allowed the opponents of Christianity to win the argument that Darwinism is science, that it has dispensed with the need to believe in God the creator and that we must make up our own morality. We have allowed them to win the argument that our state of scientific knowledge makes us competent to lay down the optimum relationships between man and man and that, in this way, we will eventually find ways of dealing with antisocial behaviour. We have allowed them to remove the absolute categories of right and wrong, of crime and punishment, and to put in their place the idea of cures for diseased conduct. The man in the white coat has taken the place of the judge and man's dignity as a responsible creature is removed. Faced with the monstrous rise in the statistics of what is still admitted as crime, they have ignored them, denied their validity and when they show no sign of coming down, have pleaded for more time and more figures. Their slogan is freedom, but their sin is the original sin of wanting to be gods and to decide for themselves what is right and what is wrong. The result is a great loss of real freedom and a rise in human fear, loneliness and misery.

We need to fund organisations which can make the Christian case in each area of society in which Christian principles are needed to stop the rot. We also need to fund organisations which can conduct the research needed to maintain a steady overall campaign. And we will find that we are not alone. Each campaign will bring allies who may not be Christians, but who represent those who are being hurt by what has gone wrong. In the campaigns against pornography, the Christians are side by side with the women's movements. In the campaigns against abolition of all restraints on Sunday trading, the Christians were greatly helped by the trade union movement, the small shopkeepers and, eventually, by the big stores. And there is still a big majority in the country who want to see stability in family life.

I believe that the most urgent need is to protect the family, which is under attack on all fronts. But rather than tackle each separate attack on the family, only to find ourselves, in each case, answered by a plea for personal freedom, Christians should mount a campaign for the family itself. The social statistics show how much it is under threat and opinion polls show that it is still a most popular institution for which there is no substitute. The great majority want the security of marriage and do not marry with the intention of divorcing. TV advertisements still show a typically happy family, reflecting what most people believe is the optimum way of life. We want all the separate attacks on society to be seen for what they are, a danger to the happiness and health of society. Instead of the 'pro life' campaign being a head-on clash between Christians and the women's liberation movement, leaving Christians arguing with each other about whether the foetus has a soul, we can begin to ask questions about the effect on society of a rate of abortions which has reached one to every five live births, of the effect on children of one-parent families and of a succession of step-fathers or step-mothers. The Christian must promote a concept of a healthy and a whole society in order successfully to oppose each of the demands for rights coming from this group or that.

There should be no doubt, as we look at the disaster facing our confused society and at all the moral issues on which we have clear Christian teaching, that some of our giving should go to support those who are arguing the Christian case. We are not a club or a sect. The Christian church is two thousand years old, it has a long casebook of the moral issues with which it has had to deal, its successes and failures are heavily documented. But we also believe in a God who has not only made us, but who has given us the maker's handbook. Above all, we believe in a God who will judge each of his rational creatures by the law which he has given. So we owe a duty to our neighbours which we cannot avoid to tell them what that law is.

13   How should we give?

The style of our giving matters

There is no question of style in writing out a cheque for the
heating bill. We either do it or we don't. But giving to God
is different. The way we do it matters. Paul tells the
Corinthians that they must give generously, gladly and
gratefully.

We should give generously

In 2 Corinthians 9:2, Paul talks of the Corinthians' eager-
ness and enthusiasm. Whatever the other faults of the
Corinthian church, they are generous. Paul wants to see
that this enthusiasm is translated into hard cash on the
actual day of collection and asks them to have the money
ready ahead of time, so that 'it will be ready as a generous
gift, not as one grudgingly given' (2 Cor 9:5). He goes on to
explain, 'Whoever sows sparingly will also reap sparingly,
and whoever sows generously will also reap generously' (2
Cor 9:6). The nineteenth-century American theologian
Charles Hodge comments, 'The reluctance spoils the gift
. . . Unless we feel it is an honour and a joy to give, God
does not accept the offering.' That is a sobering thought.

But if we are generous with God, he has promised to be
generous with us. Proverbs 11:24,25 says: 'One man gives
freely, yet gains even more; another withholds unduly, but
comes to poverty. A generous man will prosper; he who
refreshes others will himself be refreshed.' Proverbs 22:9
says, 'A generous man will himself be blessed, for he shares

his food with the poor. Christ himself says, 'Give, and it
will be given to you. A good measure, pressed down,
shaken together and running over, will be poured into your
lap. For with the measure you use, it will be measured to
you' (Lk 6:38).

Natural wisdom tells us that the more we give, the poorer
we will be. Divine wisdom tells us the opposite. It is part of
the principle laid down by Christ, 'whoever wants to save
his life will lose it, but whoever loses his life for me and for
the gospel will save it' (Mk 8:35). The divine principle is that
the generous and cheerful giver will always have something to give and that generous giving is not the way to
poverty, but to increased wealth. This is because God the
creator of all things is able to 'make all grace abound'.

Psalm 112 expresses the divine wisdom most clearly:

Blessed is the man who fears the Lord,
who finds delight in his commands.
His children will be mighty in the land;
the generation of the upright will be blessed.
Wealth and riches are in his house,
and his righteousness endures for ever.
Even in darkness light dawns for the upright,
for the gracious and compassionate and righteous man.
Good will come to him who is generous and lends
    freely,
who conducts his affairs with justice . . .
He has scattered abroad his gifts to the poor,
his righteousness endures for ever;
his horn will be lifted high in honour.
The wicked man will see and be vexed . . .
the longings of the wicked will come to nothing.
    (Ps 112:1–5,9,10)

But this does not justify the American cult which encourages its followers to pray for riches. The riches of the
righteous man in the Psalms are the result of his generosity,
not of his insistence that he is entitled to them by his

righteousness. If the Christian is rich, it is a by-product of his obedience. The Christian must never aim for riches as an end in themselves. Paul warns us that 'People who want to get rich fall into temptation and a trap and into many foolish and harmful desires that plunge men into ruin and destruction. For the love of money is a root of all kinds of evil' (1 Tim 6:9,10).

There is a tendency for evil to produce misery and poverty and for good to produce peace and plenty. One is destructive, the other constructive. There is a tendency for the hardworking, honest and trustworthy to prosper and even in this life, the good man will be happier than the bad. But in both the Old and New Testaments we also read of the prosperity of evil men and of the persecution and suffering of good men, whose only reward is in heaven.

So the divine truth we are taught is simply that we will not suffer from our generosity, quite the contrary. God, who is the giver of all, will look after those who gladly, cheerfully and generously look after others.

We should give gratefully

We should also give gratefully. Paul ends the passage on giving in 2 Corinthians by speaking of 'the surpassing grace God has given you' (2 Cor 9:14) and then exclaims, 'Thanks be to God for his indescribable gift!' (2 Cor 9:15). It is generally agreed that, especially in that context of God's surpassing grace, the only gift which can be called 'indescribable' is the gift of his own Son for our redemption.

In every other religion mankind is told to work for its own salvation. Only the Christian faith dares to tell of God almighty, the Creator of the universe, holy and just, helping to find a way back for his rebellious creation. He does this by coming in the person of God the Son and himself suffering the punishment for our rebellion. The truth of revealed religion is stranger than the fiction of invented religion. Mankind knows that there has to be punishment for rebellion. But, left to ourselves, we will not accept that it is impossible for us to purge our rebellion by ritual gestures. No human religion would dare to teach that God himself would take the punishment, that God the Son would be separated by the sin of our rebellion from God the Father and that the gift of forgiveness cannot be bought, rather it is absolutely free. That is the good news of the Christian faith, the gospel preached by the apostles and by the evangelists of the church ever since.

So every gift the Christian brings to God has to be a gift of gratitude for the great gift God has given to us. He has not only given us life, food, home, family, beauty and friendship, he has given us through the sacrifice of Christ the hope of eternal life with himself, a life in which the first destiny of mankind, fellowship between the creature and Creator, will be finally fulfilled. At present we can only imagine it in negative terms – no pain, no evil, no ageing, no boredom, no weariness, no hunger. Or we can see the relationship only in terms of imagery – of the church as the bride and Christ as the bridegroom, of the touching language of the Song of Solomon. But however we see it, Christians who know what it is to have received the peace of God's forgiveness and who remember the death of Christ at every Communion service, must feel an overwhelming gratitude which puts into perspective the small gifts that are all we can give in return for the greatest gift of all.

We must give privately

In the sermon on the mount Christ told his followers that we were to give privately. He said,

> Be careful not to do your 'acts of righteousness' before men, to be seen by them. If you do, you will have no reward from your Father in heaven. So when you give to the needy, do not announce it with trumpets, as the hypocrites do in the synagogues and on the streets, to be

honoured by men. I tell you the truth, they have received their reward in full. But when you give to the needy, do not let your left hand know what your right hand is doing, so that your giving may be in secret. Then your Father, who sees what is done in secret, will reward you. (Mt 6:1–4).

Jesus also said that, as part of the same principle, prayer and fasting should be in secret. We must remove completely the temptation to parade our spiritual actions in order to receive worldly applause. We may not expect much worldly applause today for prayer and fasting. But there is still plenty of worldly recognition of generous giving. Charities frequently publish lists of donors and, at the top end of the scale, governments give honours for those who have given some of their huge fortunes to charitable causes. But, for the Christian, Christ prescribes oblivion, 'Do not let your left hand know what your right hand is doing.'

As we catch a ball, our hands come together in perfect synchronisation. Each hand knows exactly what the other is doing. So Christ can only mean that we not only do not advertise our giving in any way, but that we forget about it as soon as it is done. We forget about a garage bill as soon as we file away the receipt. There is nothing more boring than a pile of old bills. But we are tempted to feel that someone still owes us something for our giving and we remember it long after it is done. And we still want to feel the warm glow of approval. But God owes no one. He gave us 100%. We have only given back a fraction. And he has given us more than money. So we must put it behind us at once.

In the parable of the sheep and the goats in Matthew 25, the righteous are amazed when they are asked to take their inheritance. They cannot remember that they have done anything to deserve it. They ask, 'Lord, when did we see you hungry and feed you, or thirsty and give you something to drink? When did we see you a stranger and invite you in, or needing clothes and clothe you? When did we see

you sick or in prison and go to visit you?' (Mt 25:37–39). It is
the self-righteous who point out all that they have done and
the king has to point out their neglect of the hungry, the
thirsty, the sick and the stranger (Mt 25:41–46).

We know that Christ also tells us to let our light shine
before men (Mt 5:16). But it is better that the light of
generosity should be the light of the whole church. The
more the giving is associated with the church collectively,
the more it is attributed to the Christian faith and the less to
our individual merit. Of course the church's care for those
who need help will be known. But it will reflect to the merit
of the Christian church and not to the merit and importance
of particular rich donors.

Also, there are gifts of which the world warmly approves
and there are gifts which it thinks a waste of money. The
best way to avoid being influenced by the likelihood of
worldly approval is to keep our individual giving private.

Although we are not to look for the reward for our giving
on earth, there is a heavenly reward. There are some people
who think we should do good for its own sake and that it is
unspiritual to think of any reward at all. But we are told in
Hebrews 12:2 of 'Jesus . . . who for the joy set before him
endured the cross'. If it is right for Jesus 'the author and
perfecter of our faith' to make the greatest sacrifice of all 'for
the joy set before him', it cannot be wrong for us to act for
eternal reward.

Jesus tells us to lay up treasure in heaven, where neither
moth nor rust corrupt and where thieves do not break in
and steal (Mt 6:20). The clear implication is that what we
give here, we will receive back there.

We should give prayerfully

Just as we say, 'Why stay on your knees asking God when
you can also go out and do something yourself?' so when
we give, we should also pray. When the offering is taken up
to the front in church, we pray that God will use our gifts.

So we should also pray for God's blessing when we give individually. The causes and the people to whom we give should be on our prayer list. If they are worth giving to, they are worth praying for. If we pray thoughtfully and intelligently, we can hardly fail to give with more thought and intelligence. As we pray for a cause, we realise that we could help with money too. We pray for someone who is ill and wonder whether we could do something for their family. So, as we pray we begin to see where our priorities should lie.

Not only do we speak to God in prayer, he speaks to us. When we get down on our knees to God almighty and pray for something trivial and unworthy, he makes us realise that it *is* trivial and unworthy. It is on our knees that we see our lives in their true context. We are reminded of what is really important and what is not, we see what is pure selfishness and what is true neighbourly love and care. You cannot lie to God; so our self-delusions wither as we try to articulate them. We are shown that we are here to serve God and not to serve ourselves. We see that one gift we had thought of is self-serving and another is purely sentimental. We see that in another, we are being carried away by the crowd in a tide of emotion and excitement.

We should give thoughtfully and unsentimentally

It is clear from the Bible that animals are part of God's creation, that they are dependent on us and that we must not be cruel to them. So animal welfare is a legitimate Christian concern. We should not ill-treat them so that their meat tastes better. But we also have to keep down animals which are predators on our food stocks. If the seal population goes up too fast, the fish population can be damaged, so seals are culled. But baby seals are also killed for seal-skins and, though God clothed Adam and Eve with skins, there are those who believe that the culling of baby seals is excessive, as well as cruel.

Whatever the merits of this case, one of the most expensive campaigns I have ever encountered was the campaign in the European Parliament against the culling of baby seals. The campaigns for human rights are waged on cheap cyclostyled paper and are reasoned arguments based on personal cases which are put together with great difficulty and at considerable personal risk. The campaign against culling was based on a series of extremely expensive books of glossy photographs of baby seals, wide-eyed and appealing, sent to every member of parliament, on huge advertisements in all the European press and in a write-in campaign of over half a million letters. I saw no reasoned argument about the relative sizes of fish population and seal population. These were given us by a visiting delegation of members of the Canadian Parliament who would have to fund the needed seal-culling operations without the by-product of the sale of sealskins. And the majority of the letters we received were strongly motivated by the pictures of baby seals alone.

I am not saying that the case was wrong. Some of my colleagues voted against it in protest at the style and, above all, at the cost of the campaign. I was finally persuaded by letters from the Congress of the United States, which had already banned the import of sealskins. Seal-culling would go on, but would be limited to the need to conserve fish stocks. But I can think of a hundred causes put to us before and since which could have done wonders with a fraction of the money devoted to the saving of the seals.

We should give regularly

I have served on finance committees of Christian movements for over thirty years and have been the treasurer of the International Fellowship of Evangelical Students for six years. There is nothing more that a Christian organisation – or any other charity – values than the steady, reliable donor. When you have a bad month you begin to think of all your field staff thousands of miles away from home and of all the people who, in turn, depend on them. You calculate on the number of weeks' pay which you can meet from the reserves. You cancel a conference which has been a year in preparation and put another on standby. You cancel much-needed visits and stop recruiting. Time and energy turn from the proper work to fundraising.

It is the donor who stays with the movement year-in and year-out who saves a movement from these debilitating financial crises and who enables a movement to operate with minimal reserves. It is the long-term, well-informed donors who keep the fundraising cost to a single-figure percentage of the income. It is their regular monthly cheques which keep the income from bouncing about so alarmingly. To all treasurers, regular donors are the salt of the earth.

At the other end of the scale is the donor who gives to the flavour of the month. A great mission with a star international speaker will take three months' donations. A personable missionary speaker, painting a vivid picture of her work, will take two months'. The 'adoption' of an African orphan who writes letters back will take another month's. A TV appeal for the victims of a natural disaster will take another, until less than half a year's donations are left for the local church, all the local causes and overseas missionaries.

There is nothing more depressing on a visit to the United States than to watch the expensive TV fundraising spots and to realise that an enormous proportion of the giving is going to causes which spend half or more of their income on TV advertising. We watched one service in which a famous preacher spent more time in promotion than he did in preaching. In appealing for his seminary, he produced a student who was every mother's boy, clean, polite and white. He said nothing about the seminary. The student was the message. And even the student himself was not allowed to say much. He seemed to be there mostly to smile and be seen.

Another even more depressing TV spot showed
'missionaries' handing out leaflets to junkies in Hong Kong.
Then a print-out chart showed the names of those who had
filled in the form at the bottom of the leaflet and it was
implied, though not said, that the names were those who
had made a commitment to Christ. The presenter gave the
cost to the organisation of each 'commitment' and asked the
viewers to send that amount 'to save a soul'. The camera
switched to a bank of telephones with pretty girls waiting to
receive callers' gifts and credit-card numbers and then back
to the presenter for a final emotional appeal.

This form of advertising depends on uncommitted
money being available for the most appealing and the most
sensational bidder, regardless of the real merits of the case,
of the cost of raising it on TV and of the needs of those who
are much more careful with the money they are given. It is
small wonder that the cults are flourishing!

We should give responsibly

Christ teaches us in his parables that we are only stewards
of what God has given us. The master in the parable returns
and holds his people responsible for what they have done
with all he gave into their charge. The parable of the talents
(Mt 25:14–30) and the parable of the pounds (Lk 19:11–27)
are about more than money, but the gift of money is the
basis of the illustration and in neither parable is it enough
for the servant to account for the exact sum given. The
servants also were held to account for its fruitful use. So we
will surely be held to account for the way we give and we
must see that our money is given to the best possible
causes.

It is not easy for all of us to do this. We are not all experts
in Christian work. We do not all have lists of possible
causes. We cannot all read their accounts and evaluate their
work. But we can all try to see that our giving is handled by
those who can.

There are powerful arguments for channelling most of our giving through the church. The church should have a better flow of information about the different needs locally, nationally and internationally. It should have more expertise in assessing them and in deciding on priorities. If everyone gave through the church, giving would be less vulnerable to the salesmanship, pressure and sentimental appeals brought to bear on the individual donor. Paul's appeals for money were made to the church collectively and the credit which then went to the church is today dispersed over all the individual Christian donors.

One big church of which we were members used to have an 'annual appeal for special funds' which they used for all outside donations to home missions. 90% of the ordinary Sunday collection then went to the church's own needs and 10% to overseas missions. The church believed in regular giving and there was not much change from year to year in the causes to which it gave, but there was an annual discussion among the church leaders on new needs which had come up. Although the annual appeal was substantial, I am sure that a good many people did not trust all their giving to the church and I am quite sure that there is an even greater proportion of donors in smaller churches who will not channel their giving through the church.

This is often because the church itself does not feel able to handle all the donations of their members. There can be a great deal of time-consuming paperwork involved but there are trusts, such as the Charities Aid Foundation in Britain, who have the expertise to handle the tax and will do all the paperwork on their computer at little cost.

However, many churches do not feel that they even have the experience needed to assess the different needs. Very often they are right. There is no 'consumer's guide to missions'. Missionary magazines tell us very little. How can they? They are operating, with permission, in foreign countries. Their position is increasingly fragile. They cannot criticise the corruption of the host country, the superstition of its religions, its rigid caste system or its

treatment of women. They do not want to talk about
missionary wastage or, except in general terms, about
culture-shock. The stresses and strains between missionaries living together in a difficult climate far from home are
left for the occasional daring book. The very real clashes of
view on the best policies for the mission are dealt with even
more obliquely. It is not the job of the donor to manage the
mission, but those who have to decide where scarce resources are most wanted need to know more than they do
now.

There has been a great deal of concern among those
responsible for food aid about the amount which goes
astray, ending up in the bazaars to be bought by those who
can afford it – while the really needy still starve. So, as
mentioned above, there has been a conscious shift to giving
through non-governmental agencies (NGOs), who can, if
they are not satisfied, refuse a host government without creating far-reaching diplomatic and political shock-
waves.

But governments and federal agencies need to know
what is happening to public money. So there is a well-
informed dialogue not only at the formal level between
the NGOs and governments, but between NGOs and the
political leaders on the development committees of, for
instance, the US Congress and the European Parliament.
The problems of bribery, of diversion of supplies, of civil
disorder and civil war, of tribal jealousies, of undue dependence on food aid are all well understood and policies
have to take them into account. The need for capital investment in farming, for irrigation, education, transport, ferti-
liser plants and research into local crops and local diseases
are all well ventilated.

We need some such breath of free discussion blowing
through the work of mission and the creation of an
informed opinion between missions and with those
who fund them. The missions know all about the problems,
but they have no forum in which to discuss the issues
realistically with donors.

Perhaps the best model would be to set up local advisory groups of compatible churches who could discuss priorities in giving with each other and to whom both overseas and home missions could relate, as could any other causes which felt that they should be able to call on the churches for funds. Each advisory group should be able to call on experienced volunteers within the area to act as a secretariat, keeping in touch with the missions and charities and putting forward their findings for discussion with the advisory group. No individual church need be bound by an advisory group, but the arrangement would give the churches far better information on which to make up their own minds as to where their priorities lay.

For instance, six churches with similar bases of faith might initially list the causes to which they currently give, showing what proportion of their total giving each cause receives, and also the reasons why they give to each particular cause. They might then ask their secretariat to set out the bare details of each of the causes to which any church gives – how many people the cause employs, its latest annual income, its cost of administration as a percentage of its income, and a brief account of its work. Even these bare bones would give each church a great deal more information than the elders and deacons would normally have in deciding on the allocation of funds, and would raise questions and give new ideas about each church's own giving.

But the comparison of past patterns of giving would be the least of the benefits. An active advisory group could look at the needs of the city rather than at the needs of the parish or church district. And wherever there was a need which they believed the churches could and should meet, they could go back to their own churches and put it to them. The collective giving would not only ensure that the need was met, but the collective witness of so many Christians in that city would be far greater than the witness of any one church acting on its own. We may have different forms of service and methods of church government, but our coin is of the same currency. Yet all of this activity is voluntary and leaves each church with full autonomy.

It would also be possible for the advisory group to take an intelligent interest in all the causes to which they subscribe. Overseas missions cannot publish much about the problems they face in the countries in which they work. And good missions, at home and abroad, hesitate to publish personal accounts of those who turn to the mission for help. But a group advising a number of churches in a city or county can develop personal contact with missions and then have a far better feeling for their work and needs. This knowledge is then available for the elders and deacons who are responsible for the funds of each church. Both as a treasurer of a mission and as a church member, I should find this sort of two-day exchange a tremendous help.

The advisory group might also fund an office with a small computer which could handle on their behalf all the paperwork which smaller churches find they cannot handle themselves. It might also be easier to persuade church members to bring all their giving within the church if those who were most experienced were co-opted on to a board with some of the church leaders and the board made responsible for handling the church's giving to outside causes.

There is little doubt that if all church members tithed their income and gave it to the church to handle, few churches would at present be able to deal with the flow of money which resulted. That increase would force all churches to think of new ways of dealing with this side of the church's ministry.

Finally we live in a world which is increasingly corrupt. It is absolutely essential that the church accounts fully for all the money it has received. There is a wonderful early Charlie Chaplin film where Charlie, on the run from the cops, takes refuge in a church service and finds himself taking up the collection. He follows the sole deacon into the vestry and is outraged to find him stuffing his own pockets. Between the deacon and the cops Charlie has a hard time, but I seem to remember a shot of the deacon disappearing down the road with the church in full pursuit. Churches owe it to the good name of their officers to make sure that no one can raise a complaint or accuse an officer about the way in which the church's money is handled.

Conclusion

I hope that this book has been a help to the reader. Of course it runs counter to the spirit of the age, which emphasises rights rather than duties, leisure rather than work, and receiving rather than giving. But Christ told us, 'Whoever finds his life will lose it, and whoever loses his life for my sake will find it' (Mt 10:39).

So however tough the Christian way may seem, no one who takes it ever has any regrets. Older Christians looking back down the steep and narrow path they have climbed, can see that there was no other way, and that if they had to do it again, they could not choose any other path. This is not the self-justification of old age. Old age can also be a time of bitter regret and recrimination. It can see the time wasted in useless occupations, the talents squandered and the money misspent. But when Christians look back, they can see, in retrospect, the hand of God guiding and guarding; they can see a plan and a purpose to their lives.

The apostle Paul had a hard life. He tells us:

Three times I was beaten with rods, once I was stoned, three times I was shipwrecked, I spent a night and a day in the open sea, I have been constantly on the move. I have been in danger from rivers, in danger from bandits, in danger from my own countrymen, in danger from Gentiles; in danger in the city, in danger in the country, in danger at sea; and in danger from false brothers. I have laboured and toiled and have often gone without sleep; I have known hunger and thirst and have often gone without food; I have been cold and naked. Besides everything else, I face daily the pressure of my concern for all the churches (2 Cor 11:25–28).

But he also tells Timothy

. . . the time has come for my departure. I have fought the good fight, I have finished the race, I have kept the faith. Now there is in store for me the crown of righteousness, which the Lord, the righteous Judge, will award to me on that day – and not only to me, but also to all who have longed for his appearing (2 Tim 4:6–8).

Pioneer missionaries speak in the same spirit. Looking back over their lives they remember the danger, the squalor, the loneliness, the illness; but above all else, they remember the people who have come from darkness to light, whose whole lives have been transformed, together with the lives of their families. Where once there was terror and superstition, now there are lively, loving churches. It was God's work, but they were God's instruments, and how could they regret what he enabled them to do?

The decision to begin to use our time, talents and money in the way that we should is not a light decision, but it is not a heavy one either. If we are in any doubt, we should simply try it out. It can certainly do us no harm to begin to organise our time. At the very least it would be interesting to find out where it all goes. Nor can it do us any harm to start to use our talents better, and to discover how they grow. And finally it would really cost us very little to discover whether in tithing our income we were any worse off. As Malachi said to the Jews, '"Test me in this," says the Lord Almighty "and see if I will not throw open the floodgates of heaven and pour out so much blessing that you will not have room enough for it"' (Mal 3:10).

No man is an island, and the more members of the Christian church take their faith seriously, the more impact that church will have in our society. Politics alone cannot stop the rot in our society. It can bind the wounds and tidy up afterwards. It can toughen up on law and order. But the politician alone cannot stop endemic moral corruption, the break-up of the family, the toleration of mass unemployment, and the rising tide of violence without a change in moral values. I am in favour of binding up the wounds and doing whatever a politician can do – and much more could be done. But politicians depend on the spirit of the age, and more than political rhetoric is needed to change that spirit.

More than religious rhetoric is needed too. It will need more than words to get the majority of our people past a church door. It will need action. That action starts with the individual Christian. If we really care about our neighbours, care about their material needs as well as their spiritual, then they may begin to listen. If each of us, as Christians, uses all our time, talents and money as we should, the Christian church will be able to show Christian love for the needs that people feel most acutely. If we care for the needs they feel and know about, they may then begin to believe us when we tell them of the spiritual needs which they have but do not know about. The Christian faith is not just a club which wants more members. We believe that we have been entrusted with a message from a just but loving God to his rebellious people. We have an overriding duty to pass on that message of justice and love. We have to tell of the judgement which must come from God's justice, of the salvation which he offers in his love, and if we want our neighbours to listen we must show them God's justice and love expressed in our own lives.